THE UNBREAKABLE RULES OF MARKETING

THE
UNBREAKABLE
RULES
OF MARKETING

9 ½ WAYS
TO GET PEOPLE TO LOVE YOU

CATHEY ARMILLAS & JEFF BERRY

Published in the United States by Chili Bomb Press
Chili Bomb and Chili Bomb Press are trademarks of Chili Bomb Press, LLC.

Chili Bomb Press, LLC
P.O. Box 23932, Tigard, Oregon USA 97281

ISBN 978-0-9850054-0-5

Cover photo: Jeffrey Freeman, www.jeffreyfreeman.com
Cover design: Ranilo Cabo
Layout design: Dave Barcos, www.remedydesigngroup.com
Editing: Sheryl Brodie and Karin Kusumakar

CONTENT

WHAT THE HELL?

IS THIS BOOK FOR ME?

Are you reading this sentence without moving your lips? Then, the short answer is, yes, this book is for you. It's not just for marketing pros. It's for all sentient beings (even those who listen to abridged books on their mobile devices while at the gym). That's because every multi-cellular life form, whether aware of it or not, is in an almost constant state of marketing. We're marketing ourselves, our opinions, our causes, our businesses, our availability for mating, our rightness for a job, or our deserving of your vote all the time. We're social animals. And that makes us marketing animals.

Everyone has a vested interest in marketing because everyone indulges in it. We're not just talking about TV commercials and selling stuff. Marketing behavior permeates every waking moment of your life. If you take the time to get dressed in the morning, you're marketing yourself to everyone you interact with that day. You market yourself whenever you speak, in how you stand and walk, where your eyes are when you talk to someone, in whether you cross your legs or not when you sit. When you shop in a supermarket, you're swimming in marketing. If you drive down the street, you're being affected by marketing messages in every other car you see, every sign you ignore, and every pedestrian with a slogan on their shirt or butt.

Ever try to impress a new acquaintance at a party with your witty banter or your cologne? You're marketing yourself. Ever try to ask someone out on a date, or manipulate them into asking you out? You're marketing. Ever try to persuade a friend over to a certain political view? Marketing. Ever interview for a job? Marketing. Ever try to get your kids to at least try a new, healthful food on their plate before they get dessert? Marketing. In fact, everything we do that involves an interaction with another thinking, feeling life form is marketing.

Ultimately, marketing is what you do to get people to love you. Marketing is persuasion. It's getting someone to act, think, or relate to you in a desired way. That's all it is. And it's something we all do, even if only subconsciously. But being aware of it will make you more effective at getting people to act, think, or relate to you in that desired way. That's why we wrote this book; to help you be more aware.

So even if you're not the VP Chief Marketing Officer of YoYoDyne Propulsion Systems, even if you've never tried to market a business, this book and its 9½ Unbreakable Rules are for you.

And oh, yes, there are rules.

RULES? IN A KNIFE FIGHT?

Marketing often does feel like a knife fight, or at least an analog for war. It's like war in that you are constantly focused on seizing your competitor's customers, expanding your market share, and (in the words of philosopher Genghis Khan) riding their horses and burning their cities (well, maybe not the latter two). Marketing is also in getting that job, winning over that certain someone, or getting your candidate elected. Competition, whether in business or social behavior, is a fact of life. The fight never ends.

Also, adding to the mayhem, new technology is constantly upsetting everything. Thirty years ago, just as humanity had finally figured out how to use the once-novel medium of broadcast television, along came cable. And just as we all got used to how to incorporate cable in our media options, along came the Internet. And then social networks. And Twitter. And whatever next pops up this year.

But the thing that never changes, regardless of whatever new medium presents itself, is that fundamental purpose of marketing: persuasion. And one of the first things you have to do to start persuading is to get attention, which you can't seem to do unless you break some rules. So why should there be rules in the first place?

Well, there *are* rules. Any human activity needs rules, even if those rules seem so inherent they're virtually invisible. Rules govern everything. Otherwise it's just chaos and broken glass everywhere. In fact, you can't even break the rules unless there are rules to break.

That's why whether you're a professional marketer,

business owner, or just a person interested in how marketing affects you, you need to understand the 9½ Unbreakable Rules of Marketing. Because if you're going to be good at either selling a new brand of handheld gizmo or just getting that cute guy in your yoga class to notice you, you need to embrace them—the rules, not the cute guy, necessarily.

Most of us hate rules. They make us bristle. They challenge our instincts to be free. Tell us a rule and we reflexively start figuring out a loophole to get around it. Creativity, which is one of the Unbreakable Rules of Marketing (Rule #3, in fact), depends on doing things differently, and often breaking the rules. Doing things differently stands out. And standing out is good—at least in marketing. Apple co-founder and iconic rule-breaker, Steve Jobs, said it best when, in influencing the way everyone related to technology, he told us all to "Think different." In other words, break the rules. (Including the rules of good grammar; it's "differently", Steve.)

So what the hell? A rule says you have to do things the same way every time. Nobody who follows rules will stand out. So it seems like following rules would work against good marketing. No?

No.

Rules are actually useful in an activity that demands creativity, especially in knowing when you're breaking one. Rules keep you in the arena when you're playing. They establish recognizable goals. They tell you when you've won. Without rules, everything is chaos. And if everything is chaos, nothing has a chance to stand out. So you need some rules, if for nothing else, to create a field of reference against which your wacky ideas can bloom. But this is more philosophical than we wanted to get. We just want to tell you how to get that date, or that job, or sell your handheld gizmo.

WHERE DO THESE RULES COME FROM?

A fair question. As far as we know, they aren't written down in any coherent college text, though most of them do appear in one form or another in various marketing courses. One of the reasons we decided to write them down and number them was because, while we've been following them for decades ourselves, and learned them from our own mentors, they haven't been written down. They seemed so basic that nobody ever saw the need to. It's like writing down the rules of breathing. They are so basic they should be instinctive. We've both automatically applied them to the work we do for our own clients. We've observed them in action in other marketing campaigns, either in the observance or breach. And we've even taught them in college courses ourselves. But we've never written them down for future generations to follow. So we thought, "What the hell! Let's do it!"

We also have a noble mission. We've both been in marketing long enough to see that we have a responsibility to our grandchildren to keep them from getting sloppy. Discipline erodes. Money is wasted. Standards slide. We owe it to the kids to keep marketing from going all to hell. We're saints that way.

So, in writing this book, we wanted to remind people that marketing—even if you're just marketing yourself—stands on a solid platform of rules. These rules have always been with us, handed down on tablets from someplace mythical and high up, and passed on from generation to generation.

Some of these rules are so intuitive that it feels almost unnecessary to have to write them down (like Unbreakable Rule #3, Be Creative or Die).

Others are counter-intuitive (like Rule #1, Consistency Beats Ability) and seem, on the surface, to fly in the face of conventional wisdom—which should, ironically, appeal to the unconventional among you.

All of the rules are inter-related. For instance, getting your customers to love you (Rule #6) requires communicating on an emotional level (Rule #7) which means altering someone's reality by changing their perception (Rule #2) with creativity (Rule #3), and so on. It's a lot of chainsaws to juggle. But after juggling them for awhile they become second nature. And you'll forget the chain saws are running.

WHO ARE THESE RULES FOR AGAIN?

Everybody. You don't have to be in marketing to apply them, or even in business. As we elaborate in Rule #9, everything is marketing. It's not just for business. Teachers are marketing when they are trying to keep their students on the edge of their seats learning a new idea. A teenager is marketing when trying to get into an exclusive clique. A politician is marketing when trying to win votes. Scientists are marketing when they are persuading colleagues to understand a new discovery, build credibility in their field, or obtain more funding. Religions market to win more converts (most religions, anyway), save souls, or keep their tax-free status. Even friends market to each other to cultivate their friendships. So the rules that apply to marketing a business also apply to living a social life.

If you are a human being, and you live with other human beings, you should pay attention to these 9½ Rules. Obey them. They're unbreakable. They apply to business, but they also apply to life.

And yes, they will be on the test.

FIRST THINGS FIRST

PUT THIS BOOK DOWN UNTIL YOU HAVE A STRATEGY

Before you dive into the Unbreakable Rules, you need to have a strategy to your marketing. You may think that the solution to your marketing is to create a new website, design a new logo, or maximize your search engine optimization. None of those are. They're just tactics. And applying tactics without a strategy is like shooting a gun into a lake and hoping you'll hit a fish.

A strategy comes in two parts, a goal and a path. In marketing the goal is always to get people to love you. It isn't to get them to buy more hamburgers or vote for you or marry you. For them to do any of those things, they have to love you first. That's your strategic goal: Get their love.

The path to that goal is the other part of strategy. The strategic path is the main message you're going to use to persuade people to love you. Do you want them to love you because you have the best customer service? Or are the most reliable? Or are tough on crime? Or will make a good mother? It doesn't matter. You just need to pick the path and stay on it.

Every one of the Unbreakable Rules in this book has to be integrated into your strategy. And without any one of them, your strategy is incomplete.

Okay, now you can read on.

UNBREAKABLE RULE #1

CONSISTENCY BEATS ABILITY

CONSISTENCY BEATS ABILITY?

"What a dumb rule!" you're probably thinking, throwing this worthless book down before you even get started. But wait, let us finish…

You are undoubtedly going to argue that a company that makes better cars, better coffee, better hamburgers, or better DVDs will certainly prevail over a rival company cranking out consistently inferior products. Wouldn't someone who is consistently bad at something fail again and again? Wouldn't a football coach who consistently runs the same play get clobbered by a more nimble coach? Doesn't someone who always plays "rock" always get beat by "paper"? And doesn't consistency also mean predictability? Well, yes.

Then there are famous historical examples where a consistent, plodding strategy defeated a more able opponent; the relentless Allies against the clearly more elite German Army in WWII, for instance. Or the North Vietnamese against the clearly more sophisticated United States in the

Vietnam War, as another example. Or, to bring up a non-military illustration, consider the triumph of Starbucks over countless other coffeehouse chains who derisively call Starbucks "bean burners."

But we're not talking about warfare, football, or caramel macchiatos. We're talking about marketing. And in marketing the inconvenient truth is that a company that is consistent with its message—even a bland message—is going to whip a competitor who changes his message with every whim, even though each succeeding message may be compelling, creative, and clever.

The rule in practice is: Pick something and stick with it.

CONSISTENCY IN IMPRESSION

Imagine how hard it would be if you were to go to work every day with a completely new face and body. Unless your job was being a spy, this shape-shifting would present incredible problems in getting to know people, in building trust, in just living. Not to mention, it would freak people out.

Now extend this problem of inconsistent appearance to a business; even your business. If your logo isn't consistent, your customers and potential customers will not know you, or trust that the communication they're getting from you is really you. The same goes for all of your graphics, your fonts, your corporate colors, even the tone of your messages. If these things are always changing, it unsettles people. And they either won't remember you or won't trust you.

This seems pretty basic. But it never ceases to amaze us

how often this basic principle of consistency is ignored by businesses, large and small. Too often, the answer to slack sales is to hire a graphic designer to change the logo, as if that itself were the magic formula that would bring in new customers. Ironically, an inconsistent impression is frequently part of a company's problem in the first place. Even something as apparently insignificant as varying typefaces on ads, brochures, or websites can do more harm to a brand's familiarity than good. The average person may not be able to identify Myriad as the corporate font of Apple, but they instinctively know that it's Apple, just as they recognize the voice of their daughter on a playground full of yelling children. If you were to start getting communications from Apple that used other fonts, you'd suspect that there was fraud afoot.

A consistent tone of voice is also important. You can tell when you get a suspicious e-mail from a friend that it really isn't them; because it doesn't sound like them. You immediately suspect that their e-mail account has been hacked. Likewise people get to know the sound of a familiar company because that company has spent years cultivating a certain voice, a personality. If that tone of voice is inconsistent, it breaks down trust. It doesn't mean that you can't change to a new voice, but the change shouldn't happen frequently, and you need to be conscious of the disconnection you're liable to cause in your audience when you do it. If you were known as a reserved person of few words, to suddenly show up at work as an overly familiar chatterbox would make people start to back uneasily away from you. Same with a business.

Consistency is also important when it comes to the frequency of the impressions you make. If you show up only occasionally, it's hard for people to get to know you. They may even stop inviting you to their parties. You're not exactly top of mind. But if you are consistent in reaching out to people, whether to your friends or your customers, you are going to build a much more solid business, or circle of friends. Of course, this sounds like advice from your mother, but your mother knew something about consistency. Most mothers do, anyway.

The main reason for being consistent is to maintain what they used to call "Top of Mind" in the branding world. Top of Mind means you are already thinking about a brand, a person, an idea, or a thing without having to go searching for it, or even being reminded of it. There are undoubtedly hundreds of brands of personal computer manufacturers in the world, but only a few come top of mind. Most people, when they are in the market for a new computer, will not search all of the hundreds of off-name brands, but will pick out the few major brands they know from familiarity and compare those. There may be some very good second and third tier competitors, but it doesn't matter. If you haven't heard of them, you're probably not going to consider them seriously.

You may acquire hundreds, if not thousands, of friends during your lifetime, but the ones you think about are the ones you see day to day, or hear from often. You're consistently connecting with them.

When you are consistent in making your impressions,

whether for personal or business reasons, you are building an army of followers. You know that when you give a party, they will come, and when you have a sale, you'll have to hire extra help to manage the crowds. But if you are inconsistent in making those impressions and you send out invitations, people are liable to say, "Who?"

CONSISTENCY IN THE SPACE/TIME CONTINUUM

The consistency principle applies in both space and time. Consistency over time is self-explanatory. It means pick a message and stick to it all year, all decade, for generations. When we think of time consistency in a brand we usually think of that brand as standing for the same thing it did our whole lives—or at least the whole life of the brand.

Coca Cola, for instance, has been around essentially unchanged since 1886. Its iconic script logo, the wave shape, and its red and white corporate colors have remained unchanged for generations. But in 1985, reacting to the famous "taste-test" challenge posed by rival Pepsi, the company experimented disastrously with changing the formula of Coke. It introduced New Coke, a sweeter, less sharp soda than the original. Coke's own blind taste tests showed that people liked it better. It sure looked like a hit.

But then something unexpected happened. Though people said they liked it in blind taste tests, the thing that Coke didn't anticipate was the intense nostalgia and brand loyalty for the old Coke. Out in the real world—the world that wasn't blind—it wasn't the taste that people reacted to and preferred, it was all the emotional equity in the idea of Coke. New Coke was a catastrophe for Coca Cola sales. People were indignant that they had been "tricked" by marketing research. They knew what they liked, and they liked Coke, old Coke.

In an effort to undo the damage of the backlash, Coke quickly reintroduced the old formula within a year, calling it Coke Classic. For a time both brands, New Coke (eventually renamed Coke II) and Coke Classic were sold side-by-side. But Coke Classic's sales soared even above its previous market share before the Cola Wars, while Coke II—the "scientifically proven" better-tasting formula—diminished to extinction (except, curiously, in Yap and American Samoa).

CONSISTENCY TRUMPED QUALITY

The New Coke cautionary tale also illustrates the second dimension of the consistency principle: space. It was not enough that Coke kept its familiar logo; over the generations it needed to maintain the formula of its actual product. Consistency in marketing even has to extend right down to the molecular level. People react to a soft drink in an almost religious way: Change its formula and they'll react viscerally, challenging their very confidence in the workings of the universe. Of course, their preference is completely subjective, but, as we'll see in Rule #2, Perception is Reality, it's still their preference.

So Coke really stepped in it when they tried to pull a fast one on its loyal customers by mucking around with the taste, even if it initially got their vote with a blind taste test. In non-blind taste tests, the loyal Coke drinker's preference immediately reverted when the liquid came out of a red and white can. Coke's attempt at changing the product formula not only backfired, the very marketing techniques themselves backfired. Fortunately, the company was savvy enough to turn the controversy to its advantage and ended up with an even greater market share by emphasizing its previous consistency—something they planned all along. Right?

This consistency in space for Coke spans the globe. In 200 countries the formula and brand of Coke is as constant as it has been for over a century. Regardless of the country, the same red-and-white script logo, the same wave swoosh, the same formula (except in the U.S., where high-fructose corn syrup is used as the sweetener instead of cane sugar), all signal a brand relationship that is shared regardless of culture or politics. Even Fidel Castro's favorite drink has been known by the CIA to be Coke; Coke Classic, of course.

The object lesson here is this: Consistency in both time and space, in advertising, graphic messaging, even in the nature of the product itself, wins out over quality. Pepsi tried to prove to people in the 1980s that their product was better when people didn't know what they were drinking. And what Pepsi found out, to their exasperation, was that people still preferred what they said they didn't prefer. It made no sense. "Coke People" liked Coke. It was the real thing.

What they were really preferring was continuity.

CONSISTENCY OF PHILOSOPHY

Consistency beats ability not just in advertising and

products, but also in philosophy, sometimes called "corporate culture". And the company that believes in its core philosophy and sticks with it will thrive.

Avis has been running its same message, "We try harder" for nearly half a century now. This message, one of continuous improvement, came out of a copy line of a single ad that appeared in 1962. The ad offered the provocative but disarming truth, "We're number 2. So why go with us?" And the answer in the first line of body copy was, "We try harder. (When you're not the biggest, you have to.)"

This argument struck home. It resonated with people who could, like nearly every living soul on the planet, identify with not being number one. They were the ordinary people, the rest of us. Moreover, everyone could identify with the virtue of trying harder. Everybody makes mistakes. Making mistakes, learning from your mistakes, working hard to improve yourself, and trying harder are all fundamental to the entrepreneurial ethic. Together they're the engine of capitalist success.

The reactions by customers to the first series of self-effacing ads was so positive that Doyle Dane Bernbach copywriter, Paula Green, who wrote the first Avis ads, insisted that "We try harder" become Avis's tagline and company mantra. She had struck a chord. Green's boss, Bill Bernbach, further insisted to Avis that the company improve themselves for real, not just in their advertising. He and the new Avis CEO, Robert Townsend, saw eye-to-eye on this; that successful marketing needed to be consistent, not just in words, but also in actions. The product needed to be as good as the promise, and the company as good as the product. "It's always a mistake to make good advertising for bad products," Bernbach was fond of saying. So if they were going to tout the "We try harder" marketing message, Avis really needed to do that in every aspect of their business; try harder.

And it did. Townsend revamped the company's entire operations to improve customer service. He established a culture of continuous improvement. Being #2 (to Hertz's #1) actually became an asset. Sticking with this message, and applying its philosophy of trying harder, Avis quickly went from being a company used to running consistently in the red, to one consistently making fistfuls of cash. Within four short years Avis increased their profits by 260% and moved from 11% to 35% market share.

Of course, "We try harder" is a timeless message. It still resonates almost 50 years later. But Townsend and successive management have taken the consistency message to heart not just in time but into every aspect of their marketing. "We try harder" permeates all aspects of the corporate culture at Avis. Every employee knows what is expected of them. Every customer knows what to expect from Avis. Every competitor knows what they are up against. Hertz may still be slightly ahead of Avis in car rentals (as of this writing, Enterprise is ahead of both of them in total revenues), but whoever is ahead is looking back over their shoulder. Tireless Avis is huffing and puffing right behind them.

The Avis philosophy is easily tested in the marketplace. A customer who has a bad experience renting from Avis is more likely to give them a break because 1) they own up to their mistakes and 2) they promise to try harder next time. An inconvenienced or disappointed customer is more willing to forgive Avis because he's been conditioned to believe they'll do better next time. He is also more willing to forgive because he knows what it's like to make mistakes, and to be #2 himself. He identifies with Avis, who still seems to be self-effacing and eager to please.

Avis never let go of that "We try harder" philosophy in favor of a momentarily "better" brand position. It's a brand promise that has worked well for fifty years, and while they have added to it and refreshed it creatively, they've stuck with it. They're the poster child of consistent marketing.

The consistent marketing message also sustains itself by driving continuous innovation. People know that Avis does not rely on past success. They know that Avis is motivated to create new ways to serve their clients, from easing the whole car rental process to anticipating their travel needs. So innovation is a natural outgrowth of this consistent marketing message.

The lesson here is also that consistent marketing extends far past a company's advertising. Advertising that is disconnected from the reality of a company's culture and operations is inconsistent marketing (see Rule #9, Everything Is Marketing). It isn't enough to make a promise; you have to follow through. You can't run an ad campaign promising hassle-free returns and then hassle customers who try to return something. You can't promise attention to detail and have sloppy manufacturing. All aspects of your brand promise have to honor that promise. Slick advertising and fast delivery of junk is still junk.

CONSISTENCY OF PROMISE: WIRELESS PHONE SERVICES

How many of us have been swayed by a clever ad campaign to try a new product only to be sadly disappointed when the promise is broken? Take wireless phone service. Each ad campaign of the major players in this highly competitive, high-turnover market promises better coverage, fewer dropped calls, and more reliability—in other words, consistency. But it seems like none of them live up to those promises. So while the advertising is all about consistency of service, the marketing and the service don't match up. You still get dropped calls. Lots of them.

This is the problem with promising something you have no control over; in this case, physics. The experience of any customer with any of today's wireless providers has more to do with the peculiarities of your environment—where you are, how your head is turned, the relative humidity that day, how close you are to metal structures—than the ability of the service provider to do something as simple as connect your phone call. You might think that here is an example where ability might be an advantage over consistency; consistently bad. If you're a mobile phone service provider, you have to have the engineering and infrastructure to handle a torrent of wireless data so you can deliver consistent services. But if you're a customer, having ten-thousand clever apps available will not make up for the fact that you can't make a reliable phone call.

Consistency needs to be not just in the marketing message, it also has to be between the promise and the delivery. The marketing decisions by the wireless providers, AT&T, Verizon, T-Mobile, and the rest, to opt for upping their offerings with sexy, data-hungry, smart phones has come at the expense of the basic phone call. Now all of them are targets for stand-up comics under the "modern problems" genre. One reason the turnover between cellular providers is so high has not been because each new phone model is so awesome; it's because the provider's service is so appalling. The technical reason, of course, is not that phone technology has lagged behind other wireless services; it's because of all of the non-voice data that's clogging up the airways. When your text message or your movie takes a little longer to download, you don't notice. But you do notice a dropped call when you suddenly find yourself talking to the air. You feel like a fool. When you ask a question and get silence, the silence is deafening.

One wonders what would have happened if AT&T (not to pick on them, but why not?), instead of signing an exclusive deal with Apple to offer the hyper-apped first iPhone, had decided to live up to its brand promise of connection reliability ("More Bars in More Places") and made sure that its network was robust enough to handle simple calls, even with the stampede of data. In other words, consistency over ability. Sure, Verizon or somebody else would have stolen a momentary march on them by having iPhones first. But then they'd be the ones comedians would be mocking. And AT&T would've been known as the steadfast provider, with more bars in more places.

But as technology advances, these relative market positions of the wireless providers also change as each one is the first to be able to offer a new, nifty feature. Of course, Verizon was soon able to take away AT&T's exclusive position with Apple and start marketing its own version of the iPhone. The only difference was that, unlike AT&T's service, Verizon's iPhone couldn't handle a phone call and data at the same time. So people couldn't check their GPS feature to see how lost they were while talking to the person they were supposed to be meeting for lunch. It was an inconvenience that Verizon seemed to dismiss as trivial when you compared the relative value of not dropping calls as frequently—until they drop your call.

BE CONSISTENTLY GOOD, NOT OCCASIONALLY EXCELLENT

Of course, consistency doesn't mean being consistently bad. What's that aphorism? Doing something over and over even when it doesn't work, but expecting a different outcome every time, is a definition of insanity—or at least obsessive compulsive disorder. The same goes for those companies who consistently do ineffective marketing and declare it "successful" simply because they haven't changed it over the years. That's insane.

It is, of course, important to find a good brand position and stick with it. Starbucks, by the estimation of coffee snobs, may not be as good as a small, locally-owned coffee bar run by people who love the art of bean roasting. But

Starbucks isn't terrible. Millions think it's pretty good, in fact. And it's consistent. When you go to a Starbucks in any airport, on any street corner, in any strip mall in the world, you have an expectation that your experience will be pretty good. The very familiarity of Starbucks itself is part of that pretty good feeling.

Another good example of a successful brand being consistently good, rather than occasionally excellent, is Southwest Airlines. Southwest flies one type of aircraft, the 737. It only flies point to point. There are no reserved seats, no first class, no frills. It's basically a bus ride in the air. And that's exactly why Southwest has consistently made a profit and survived all of the ups and downs (pun intended) that have buffeted competing airlines (the puns never stop). People know what they're getting: no surprises. Moreover, in all of its history, as of this writing, Southwest has never lost an aircraft or killed a passenger (at least while a passenger was actually seated in a Southwest airplane), a good consistency record that is more important than consistent WiFi coverage on selected flights.

We human beings tend to stick with the familiar; it makes us comfortable. Changing our brand of toothpaste every time we go to the store, or our wireless service, or even our brand of car, just takes too much mental energy. We're lazy. We don't like doing homework or making decisions that could be wrong. So if we've settled on something, and it's not going to poke our eye out, we'll probably stick with it. We're content with the familiar. In truth, it takes an enormous amount of time and energy (and a long history of bad experiences) to get us to shift from a brand we're comfortable with to another. Witness Coke's experience with New Coke.

Naturally there are exceptions. There are indeed people who love to shake up their lives, who thrive on novelty, and who feel invigorated by change. There are people who actually liked the New Coke. But these people are in the minority. And they tend to make the majority, the Coke Classic people, itchy.

Change is scary. Change takes work. Change means you're going to have to get off your couch. Change violates the Second Law of Thermodynamics. Change, whether it's learning to live with the merger of your friendly neighborhood bank into a multinational megabank, or changing your cell phone provider, is like a jarring pothole that comes out of nowhere. That's why people tend to settle for the road they're on; it may not get them there faster, but it isn't jarring their bones.

Over the past couple of decades a series of psychological studies across academia have revealed that the more choices people have, the more anxious they become (see *Scientific American*, April 2004, "The Tyranny of Choice" Barry Schwartz). Of course, there is also an unexamined belief among marketers that the more options you give people, the happier they are. But this belief is unfounded, at least for choices above two or three. Tests asking respondents to rate their sense of well-being after being presented with varying levels of choices showed that the reported sense of happiness initially rose when the choices went from zero to three, but that it started to plummet dramatically thereafter. There are some theories as to why this is, but one of the most obvious seems to be that it just takes more energy to process incoming data, and, let's face it; most people have better things to do. The brain is the most energy-hungry organ in the body. The studies have also found that the perceived consequences of making the wrong choice become magnified when the choices are plentiful. You have more chance of picking wrong. This makes having too many choices just too stressful.

This mental inertia is probably why people, contrary to what marketers seem to think, prefer consistency. Consistency has the advantage that it doesn't present them with more choices, which are stressful. They've already made a decision. And they don't want to make it again, thank you very much.

Change is also stressful because you have to process the implications of the change on your life, and that also takes work. Supermarket managers will tell you that whenever they upgrade their stores, they tend to have a fall off in old customers. Customers build up a strong relationship with their local supermarket primarily because whenever they go there they know where everything is. It's easy to shop because it's efficient, and even relaxing. But change where the milk is and you put stress on the system. You're like a brand new store to your customers. They feel disoriented. They have to build a new mental map. Suddenly you're inconsistent. Now your store is "new" to them, so those regular customers are open to try out your shiny new competitor down the street, the one with the Starbucks inside.

Of course, we're not recommending that supermarkets never upgrade their stores, or make changes to their layouts. There are other factors involved, such as the attraction of newness itself (which has its own appeal in spite of the need for consistency) or just stocking efficiency. Nor are we recommending that your company never upgrade your brand, repackage your product, or improve your marketing. But we are saying that before you make a change, make sure you're aware of the psychological effect that change will have on your loyal customers. Don't just change things because you're bored with them. Coke didn't take into account the tremendous backlash to their "improving" the formula of their flagship product. And you not taking into account the psychological power of consistency in your own business can hand you an unpleasant surprise.

HOW TO APPLY THE FIRST RULE TO YOUR OWN LIFE

Even though we've been talking about examples of consistency overcoming ability in business marketing, it also pertains to the way you live your own life. For instance, if you want to be thought of as a trustworthy person—in case you ever need to get a loan, or maybe you need someone to believe your explanation—you shouldn't get caught telling little lies or cheating. Even one lie can ruin a lifelong reputation for honesty. Percentages don't matter. Your honesty isn't graded on a curve. Someone who lies only a few times is still thought of as a liar. As we'll see under Rule #2, Perception is Reality, it's irrelevant if you statistically lie only 5% of the time, versus, say, 50% of the time. You're still known as untrustworthy. It isn't fair, maybe, but it's a fact of life. When you're playing Russian roulette, knowing that there's only one live bullet in the gun is a whole lot more unsettling than if you know there are none. In fact, it isn't even Russian roulette then.

Likewise as a parent trying to market the idea of your authority to your young children, you know it's ancient wisdom that enforcing the rules inconsistently leads to insecurity on the part of your kids. And more tantrums. When bedtime is 9 o'clock on school nights, and you occasionally let one of your kids stay up to watch a special TV program but not his siblings, you're just asking for trouble.

In sports, the athlete who consistently gives it his all, trains hard, listens to his coach, and develops a reputation for reliability on the field, is going to be far more successful than the occasional superstar who happens to be born with some talent, but only applies it when he feels like it.

And so on. The point is, overall, in all aspects of life, whether in marketing a business or living your personal life, ability's important, no question. But consistency is going to beat it in the long run.

>DO THIS

Be good at what you do, obviously.

But whatever you do, do it consistently.

UNBREAKABLE RULE #2

PERCEPTION IS REALITY

"THEY'RE IDIOTS!"

A few years ago we were attending a series of focus groups for an unnamed high-tech client. While listening to the opinions of the participants through the one-way glass, the client's product marketing director was pacing up and down, popping handfuls of trail mix, and "arguing" with what he was hearing. The focus groupees were expressing painful opinions about his product versus those of his competitor's. Their opinions were, of course, inaccurate and ill-informed—according to our client. Clearly these people didn't know what they were talking about. They were just being paid $50 to shoot off their mouths as if they were experts. And the experience of listening to this was unnerving for him.

"Don't they read the ads?" he sputtered in frustration. "I doubt they've ever even used an InterProbe 3000!" (Not the real product name, which has been changed to protect the innocent). But he was missing the point. It didn't matter if they had never used his product, or were confusing it with the competitor's, or something else; their opinions about it, however misinformed, were, for them, the truth.

The sad thing is, their perceptions are not a departure from the real world; they *are* the real world. What people believe is reality. To them. Don't confuse them with the facts.

Even scientific facts are nothing. Not unless you can get people to buy the facts. Perception is what motivates behavior, not reality.

WELL, THEN, WHO DEFINES REALITY?

The thing that you can learn from watching enough focus groups is that the "real" world is actually the "opinionated" world; the "perceived" world—at least in marketing. You can also learn a lot about a client's view of that reality from their own reactions to what's being said on the other side of the one-way window. Like most people, they will tend to cherry-pick the comments that confirm their own opinion and use that as validation.

But this principle extends beyond the artificial environment of marketing research. In all aspects of life, people form opinions and then adjust their lenses to fit the world into those opinions. We don't want to get into metaphysics here, but the concept of reality is itself just that: a concept, an opinion.

Take the last chapter's example of the fiasco of New Coke in the Cola Wars: When people realized they had been "duped" by the blind taste test into preferring the New Coke to Old Coke, they rebelled. And lashed back. Coke confused them about what they really thought. When people knew what they were drinking came out of the red and white can, it only served to confirm their previous preference.

Studies at Caltech (see Plassman, O'Doherty, Shiv, Rangel) have revealed that when wine tasters are told of the relative prices of wine in blind testing, their preferences become statistically skewed toward the ones labeled as more expensive. This was true even when the price labeling in the test was random.

In other words, it is a long understood psychological phenomenon that the experience of reality is an abstraction. It's what people perceive it to be. If they believe bad weather was caused by witchcraft, somebody's going to get burned. If they believe that those strange lights they saw in the sky last night were space aliens…well, were you there? They know what they saw.

What's going on here is that the brain is processing "objective" input into "subjective" output. People may see the truth with their own eyes, but their brains then have their own way with that truth. It's inside the brain where one develops a consensus about that "subjective" truth. The story becomes fact. They know what they saw.

Adding to this effect of the brain processing objective input into subjective judgment is a psychological phenomenon called "confirmation bias". Confirmation bias is an automatic filter you install in your brain that alerts you whenever incoming data supports your preconceived notions. So, for instance, if you believe that AT&T drops your calls more than other carriers, every time you get a dropped call on AT&T you say to yourself, "See?" If you don't believe Verizon drops calls, your little alert filter won't notify you whenever you lose a connection on your Verizon phone. It takes long and repeated experience to overcome a confirmation bias.

Look at the Bermuda Triangle. Countless statistical studies by bored math and physics graduate students have demonstrated that the likelihood of a plane crashing or boat sinking or pigs flying in that arbitrarily geographical area known as the Bermuda Triangle is no greater than in any other region of the world. There is, unquestionably, a hell of a lot of traffic passing over the BT, so planes do occasionally go down and boats do occasionally sink (no pigs have been observed to fly), but at no greater statistical rate than in the Newfoundland Triangle, or the New Jersey Triangle, or the Seattle Triangle. Yet because of widespread confirmation bias, every plane, boat, or pig that does go down between Bermuda and Miami is noticed as significant, with everyone giving each other that knowing look, and BT freaks getting out the red pins to stick in the map. "Don't confuse us with statistics. Statistics can't explain what we know we saw."

GET BACK TO MARKETING, MAN

This is all very interesting—to a sophomore in a Psych 101 class, perhaps. But what does it have to do with marketing?

To apply this to marketing, all you have to do is make sure you're in control of the story behind what people are seeing. People are going to make up a story to justify their opinion of a product or brand, so you might as well try to give them a story to begin with. You may have data on your side, but you still have to persuade people with what it all means. When Copernicus had proof that the earth went around the sun, people didn't suddenly see the truth of it; it took a couple hundred years to get it to be accepted as reality.

Apple has been a master of winning over people's perceptions. Since the introduction of the first Macintosh computer back in 1983, they have controlled the story and therefore the "truth." It is a truth, for instance, that Macs don't get viruses like PCs. It is true that Macs are easier to use. It is true that they are more robust. It is true that they are better for creativity. True for Mac owners, that is.

It is also true that they are more expensive than the average PC. But Mac owners don't care about that. In fact, the added cost serves to prove that they are right, because more expensive means better. That's just a fact. Right?

Of course, if you are a PC user, or, like us, you've used both Macs and PCs for years, often side-by-side, you tend to acquire a more balanced ("objective?") opinion of relative superiority claims. They are both just computers, household appliances, like a toaster. And both tend to get buggy over time; the result of the cold hard reality of wear and tear, and, of course, the risks of visiting unsavory websites. Macs also crash, run slowly, get hot, and tend to be subjected to all of the supposed quirkiness of PCs. But in the loyal Mac owner's mind this is never the result of a virus or design flaw. There's some other story to explain the anomaly. It was probably their own fault. Macs get old, too, after all.

When it comes to ease-of-use, that was certainly true

of the first Macs, at least compared to the old DOS-based computers of 1983. Macs *were* easier to use. That was the whole marketing genius of the first Macintosh. And that genius has continued to perpetuate that "truth", even after Microsoft has long since overtaken the Mac OS (operating system) in graphic interface. All of the advantages that Apple's OS once offered have long since been matched by the succeeding generations of Windows. Of course, now all PCs have graphic interface, including drag-n-drop. Virtually all of the mainstream creative programs developed for artists run on both platforms. Security and hygiene software cover Windows machines. In fact, many mainstream games, entertainment and business programs work only on PCs. Now whether you choose Mac or PC is just a matter of aesthetic preference—and what you call that mystical key formerly known as "Alt".

But ask an average Mac owner about his opinion of the relative merits between Macs and PCs. It's almost an article of faith to him. His perception is reality. If he starts to experience slow performance, or frequent crashing on his Mac, at least he knows it's not caused by a virus.

That's powerful marketing. People don't get nearly as excited over their loyalty to their toasters. You don't hear people describing themselves as a Black & Decker Family, or a Kenmore Family, or a GE Family, or even a Dell Family like they say they're a Mac Family. And if you dare to point out that their family Mac is just another appliance, they look at you disdainfully with that you-just-don't-get-it look.

Surprisingly, though, for all of its fanatically loyal user

base, Apple still doesn't dominate the computer market. In fact it continues to hover between 5-10% of the overall personal computer market as it has for decades now. But that's fine for Apple because the "Computer for the Rest of Us" brand position it established back in 1983 with the first Mac still serves it well. Like Avis drafting to success on "We try harder because we're #2," Apple wants its customers to think of themselves as special, "The rest of us." That 10% is solid. Their customer base is committed. And growing every year.

DON'T CHANGE THE PRODUCT, CHANGE THE CUSTOMER'S MIND

Here's another example of perception over reality in marketing: Old Spice.

Old Spice is a brand of aftershave and men's deodorant that your grandfather used to buy at what he called the "Five-n-Dime." Some of you may be old enough to remember getting it for your own dad for Christmas, mostly because that's what you could afford on your 50¢ per week allowance, and because you probably had no imagination about what else to get him when you were that age. To his generation of WWII vets, that cloyingly sweet odor of Old Spice meant something: Victory over the Axis, or possibly nostalgia for the Brooklyn Dodgers. But to his kids, that peculiar smell in the off-white bottle, and that yo-ho-ho hornpipe jingle meant just one thing: Old Spice = Old Guy.

When Procter & Gamble decided to reinvigorate this venerable brand in the face of blistering, hipper, and younger competition like Unilever's Axe Body Wash, many people probably thought they should have just put the poor old dog out of its misery. But undaunted, Procter & Gamble went to creative advertising agency Wieden+Kennedy to change people's perceptions of Old Spice. They really had nothing to lose. The current perception was awful anyway. So why not try and pump a jolt through its lifeless body?

Wieden+Kennedy came up with a creative, hilarious campaign called "The Man Your Man Could Smell Like" featuring an incredibly good-looking, bare-chested actor, Isaiah Mustafa, with a Paul Robeson baritone voice. The tone and writing were smart and satirical. The ads were silly and so infectious that they generated almost six million YouTube requests in the first 24 hours after they first aired during Super Bowl XLIV, and 40 million after a week. We will talk about the power of creativity later (Rule #3, Be Creative or Die), but in terms of changing perceptions of a product, this campaign was so powerful it turned a near-death brand into the world's number one male body wash overnight. Or at least within months. In the year after the debut of the "Man Your Man Could Smell Like" campaign, Old Spice sales went up an impressive 107%.

Of course, the stuff still smells the same as it did in 1955. It's not New Coke. But unlike Coke's misstep in the 1980s, Procter & Gamble wasn't interested in winning a blind taste (or blind smell) test: They just wanted to change the way people perceived the smell.

What Wieden+Kennedy did was equate the smell of Old Spice with hipness. They got consumers to conclude that the cloyingly sweet odor was the smell of Real Men, of virile men with a sense of humor, and so confident they could mock their own machismo. This was behavioral engineering on a vast scale. The people buying Old Spice now don't even remember (or weren't alive) when their grandfathers and great-grandfathers were slapping this stuff on their styptic-penciled cheeks. The ironic thing is that, in keeping with the consistency rule (see Rule #1), Procter & Gamble has even kept the same logo and the same hornpipe jingle tag it used sixty years ago. But now that hornpipe whistle stands for the new coolness.

CONTROL EXPECTATIONS

Macintosh computers and Old Spice are just two examples of the power of perception over reality. The world around us is thick with them. But what these two underscore is the myth of reality to begin with. Reality is a perception that everybody agrees on—or at least enough people agree on it that they can call it reality among themselves; like perceiving that the emperor has new clothes, or that something weird is going on in the Bermuda Triangle. In marketing, it isn't necessary for you to change the perceptions of everyone, just enough people to influence your sales. If you're Apple or Avis, you don't need to have a monopoly of the computer or car rental market; just a healthy, loyal market base. Like Coke, you want customers so loyal they will stick with you in spite of your competition "proving" to them that they prefer their product when they don't know any better.

So while it's important to offer quality products and

services, and while it's wise to listen to your customers, it's even more important to influence the opinions of your customers. Get control of what they expect of you. Scientific facts are nothing unless you can get people to buy the facts. Perception is what motivates behavior, not reality.

This works both ways. If you ask your customers what they want, and they want something unreasonable—say a cell phone that doesn't drop their calls—this puts you in a bind. If, on the other hand, you subtly influence what their wants should be, you can stay ahead of them, even to the extent of "over-delivering." This is called controlling expectations.

Here's an example: In-N-Out Burger is a highly successful hamburger chain that started in Southern California over sixty years ago and now spans at least six western states. In-N-Out has built a drive-through empire out of controlling expectations. For decades its slogan has been "That's what a hamburger's all about." Because that's all they make: hamburgers. It's a hamburger restaurant. Period. They don't make chicken strips, or bacon-melted anything. They don't offer healthy salads. Or breakfast. Or tacos. They just make hamburgers and fries (well, cheeseburgers, too, but do you want to quibble?). This single-minded consistency has controlled the expectations of their loyal customers for generations. Because In-N-Out is single-minded in its product offering, the perception—and the expectation—is that they must be the masters of it.

So people who are loyal customers of In-N-Out will swear that it's the best hamburger on the planet. They've been known to drive miles out of their way to find one. And you can actually see people wearing In-N-Out T-shirts in states that don't even have an In-N-Out.

What In-N-Out did right was to come up with a simple, easy-to-remember message (we just do hamburgers) and people took it from there. The chain's consistency and control of perception worked together on the customer's mind. A more methodical marketer would have had blind taste tests to demonstrate the scientific proof of superior product claims. But the ingenious marketer, In-N-Out, controlled the expectations of its customers by making an obsession with hamburgers stand for perfection. In-N-Out customers "just know." They know what they like. And they expect to like In-N-Out.

DON'T CONFUSE FACTS WITH THE TRUTH

We've already mentioned the marketing virtues of Southwest Airlines in their relentless consistency (Rule #1). But this very consistency also serves to control the expectations of Southwest's customers. They expect what they pay for.

One of the chief irritants of the airline industry since deregulation in the 1980s has been the chaos of customer service. There are so many classes of travel, so many caveats, so many problems with scheduling connections, so many variable pricing schemes that the average flyer feels like he's playing roulette every time he books a flight. Even upgrading to first class, or business class, or Executive Zinc Premiere Class, won't guarantee that he'll make his connection when he has just 15 minutes to get from Gate E37 to Gate A10 in Atlanta. In an effort to keep providing luxury services like pillows and bathrooms, airlines have had to charge for many amenities, like water and checked bags. At the same time, adding injury to insult, they've packed in seats so tight that you get a free knee dislocation with any flight greater than an hour, further hampering your ability to sprint to that next, impossible connection.

Various airlines have pointed to improving statistics in selected categories, like on-time performance and lost-baggage rates, in an effort to argue with the real-world perceptions of their customers. But in spite of all of these carefully measured statistics, one critical statistic, customer satisfaction, has been continuously dropping over the years. According to an NPR report on "Talk of the Nation" on April 4, 2011, customer satisfaction with airlines dropped a whopping 30% in 2010 alone. According to the ASCI website (American Customer Satisfaction Index), the airline industry ranked dead last among all measured sectors at the end of 2011, coming in with a 65 score (the national mean being 75.7 across all industries having customers). Even the U.S. Post Office came in at 74!

Southwest Airlines, meanwhile, by staying consistent, keeping their promises low and customer expectation realistic, has been able to weather this rising discontent with airlines in general. In fact, according to the same ACSI survey, Southwest's customer satisfaction index kept its 18-year lead in the industry with an 81 score, actually rising 2% from 2010.

People don't expect much from Southwest, so Southwest has ample opportunity to exceed their expectations. Since the airline has been able to keep its fares relatively low and rational, its regular customers expect what they pay for. They think, "It's not fancy, but it's good enough to get me there." A Southwest flyer isn't inclined to complain about the quality of her meal or WiFi connection, so she's more likely to have a favorable perception of what modest service she does get, as long as it's consistent. And to make matters even better for Southwest, they don't charge for checked bags. Airlines that do charge scored only 58 in the ACSI survey.

A large, legacy airline might protest that it's not fair; they have the data to prove they are better than Southwest. Just look at those on-time numbers and the low lost-baggage statistics!

But the perception of the flying public is reality. The typical passenger, while hearing that a certain airline loses his bags less often, knows that flying is still hell. As travel pundit Joe Brancatelli recently said on that same "Talk of the Nation" broadcast, "…if you look at the statistics, the statistics tell facts, not the truth."

CONTROL PERCEPTION, CONTROL REALITY

When you control the expectations of your customers, you control their reality. Mac users expect their machines to work beautifully, and that's what they experience. AT&T customers, on the other hand, expect their cell phones to drop calls, so every time that happens, they notice it as verifying that expectation and will tend to jump ship as soon as their "plan" runs out. Of course, Verizon customers also experience dropped calls; it's inevitable given the nature of the wireless technology. But Verizon customers are more readily forgiving because Verizon's promise is wider coverage, not fewer dropped calls. And Southwest Airline flyers are loyal because Southwest promises just the basics and never lets them down.

Who is responsible for this expectation? You are. The one on the other side of the cash register. Your customers own their perceptions. Those are their reality. They may make those perceptions up, but only out of the cloth you provide them. It's up to you to weave the cloth just so.

>DO THIS

Control your customers' perceptions, and reality will take care of itself.

BE CREATIVE
OR DIE

"DAMN IT! NOT ANOTHER COMMERCIAL! WHERE'S THE REMOTE?"

All marketing is an interruption. And nobody likes to be interrupted, especially when it's some guy trying to sell you something. Whether you're watching a TV show or reading an article or listening to music, when that ad pops up, it breaks your concentration, upsets your mood, and irritates you. So, as with any interruption, you think, "This better be good."

This is where creativity is vital. Creativity is not the frivolous decoration you hang on your marketing message to please creative directors; it is the way into the minds of your customers. Creativity is how you get their attention, hold their attention, and get them to act on your suggestion. In short, creativity is power.

Sadly, looking at the state of marketing in recent years, something seems to have been forgotten; something that was discovered back in the Golden Age of Creative Advertising in the 1960s, a principle that revolutionized marketing for a generation and was part of an explosion of economic growth and prosperity. And that principle was stated by one of the pioneers of that revolution, David Ogilvy:

"You can't bore people into buying your product."

But spend an hour today watching cable television, flipping through a magazine, or surfing the Internet (if you can limit it to that short a time) and notice how relentlessly dull and desperate the marketing messages have become in recent years. This is curious because, thanks to new interactive technology, consumers are supposed to have so much more control over what gets fed to them. They can fast forward through commercial breaks. They can close pop-ups and even block them automatically. They can use search engines to refine their shopping. They can categorize e-mails as spam even before they open them, just as they've always been able to discard junk mail envelopes proclaiming they may already be a winner.

You'd think, given the fact that human beings are masters of avoiding interruptions, that smart marketers would be even more creative to get people to pay attention to their messages. Instead they only seem to have made those messages duller and duller, making it even easier for people to resist and scan through. How often do you hear a TV spot beginning with the rhetorical question, "Paying too much for…?" Reflexively you point the remote at the screen and hit >>.

Getting people to listen to you isn't a new problem. For one thing, in spite of all the recent advances in computer technology, the one piece of software that hasn't been upgraded in a hundred thousand years is the operating system installed between our ears. Human brains still process input at the same rate we always have, back from when we were scanning the bush for saber-toothed man-eaters. Trying to concentrate on survival, people have always been resistant to interruption.

For another thing, the actual volume of input—the noise of interruption—hasn't necessarily increased in the past several decades. It may seem like it has because the channels have increased, but the receiver, the human brain, is still only processing about the same amount every day.

In the 1960s when those creative advertising pioneers like Bill Bernbach, David Ogilvy, and Mary Wells were all cutting their teeth, marketers faced the same problem of getting customers to listen to their pitches. While there were fewer media channels back then—just three TV networks and no Internet—there were, arguably, just as many marketing messages bombarding the public. A study done in the late 1960s estimated that the average consumer was assailed by as many as 5,000 marketing messages a day. Even in that Pre-Webocene Era, there were TV and radio commercials, magazine and newspaper ads, outdoor billboards, posters outside and inside buses and taxis, product placement in movies, junk mail, telemarketing, posters in airports and ballparks, and logos and slogans on the very clothes you wore. Even your high school yearbook had ads in it. In 1965, the very act of walking into a supermarket subjected you to thousands of marketing messages on every aisle. So even in that paleo-digital time, there was still a torrent of incoming marketing messages. Think about it: If you were an average person awake for 16 hours (and not living on Easter Island), you would have been processing over 300 messages per hour.

Of course, now, as in 1965, you'd be ignoring most of the interruptions. It has always been a hurricane of sell-sell-sell. If you go online to look for current estimates of marketing impressions, you get estimates of a little as 250 all the way up to 10,000 a day, depending on who's doing the reporting. In most cases we don't know how these impressions are being measured, or what is counted as an impression. But the point is there are a lot. But how many even register with you when you "see" them?

Try this experiment: Take a short trip around your neighborhood in your car, or, if you live in an urban environment, walk around the block. Count every sign you see; store signs, real estate signs, home security signs, political lawn signs, neighborhood watch signs, garage sale signs. Include every car that drives by (there's a logo on every one). Count every bumper sticker. Count everyone wearing a shirt with a logo or a brand message on it. Count everything.

We only recommend doing this experiment for a short time because it's exhausting. But you may be shocked at how often your brain is poked to process a marketing message, even when you think you're in an "ad free" environment. However, your brain has also programmed itself to filter most of them out. In fact, you'd probably only notice real estate signs if you were actually looking for a house to buy. In that case, your need adjusts the filter. For the most part, however, this noise fades into the cosmic background radiation as marketing hiss.

We have, over the years, developed clever techniques and technology to allow us to block out the noise. Even though the ability to record TV shows and fast-forward through commercials wasn't available in 1965, people still had control over what they saw. Remote controls with mute buttons had already been widely available by then. People learned that with a commercial break of 3 minutes, they had time to go to the bathroom or the kitchen. Or, worse for the marketer and the broadcaster, they could just change the channel without getting up from the couch. In reading a newspaper or magazine, people then, as now, would just flip past ads in search of an interesting article. People in 1965 were as adept at ignoring messages as we are today.

Nowadays we have technology as an ally. The advent of the DVR (digital video recorder), pop-up blocker, and spam filter helps us control what comes in. We don't even have to waste any mental energy ignoring boring interruptions. They're ignored for us automatically, without us even having to see them.

Until they invent a way to force us to watch an ad, like strapping us to a chair and Scotch taping our eyelids open (See? We just hit you with a product placement) or taking off the "skip ad" button from online pop-up ads, marketers have to figure out a way to get you to pay attention to the one message they want you to notice out of the thousands that are thrown at you every waking day. If only there was a technology that could force someone into paying attention to their message.

Ah, but there is.

FAST-FORWARD-PROOFING YOUR MESSAGE

In fact, that technology—or rather, technique—is here today. It's always been here. Bill Bernbach and that whole generation of creative thinkers discovered it decades ago and it still works. The technique is: Make 'em laugh. Be creative.

If you want to stop people from getting up to go to the bathroom just as the commercial break comes on, give them a reason to settle back in…at least for 30 seconds. Every one of us can tell when a creative ad comes on. Even today, if you're scanning at hyper-speed with your DVR remote, you can spot a funny commercial in a nano-second—and back up to watch it. You can't help yourself; creative ads just look different, even at high speed.

The 1960s saw an explosion of funny ads. Sometimes they were amusing because they were so refreshingly frank and human, like the "We Try Harder" campaign for Avis, or the early self-effacing campaigns for Volkswagen. Sometimes they were just silly, like the "I Can't Believe I Ate the Whole Thing" spots for Alka-Seltzer. Sometimes they weren't necessarily funny but still entertaining, like the famous "I'd Like to Buy the World a Coke" or "I Love New York" production numbers. What was happening was that people were sticking around to actually watch the commercials. The advertising in fashion magazines became so creative it was like fine art. People would buy and save the magazines just to look at the ads. It was often said that the ads were the most entertaining things on TV. To this day the number one reason many people say they watch the Super Bowl is for the ads. It certainly couldn't be for the half-time show. Or the football.

Creativity in marketing was discovered (or rediscovered) in the 1960s. It may have been just coincidence that this decade also saw one of the longest periods of sustained economic growth in the 20th century. Or it may have been that the economic boom of the '60s itself allowed for a creative revolution in marketing. But the purpose of this book isn't economic theory.

The principle that a marketing message had to be creative became an Unbreakable Rule. In short, creativity was not an option: It was mandatory. This principle prevailed as common industry knowledge for at least thirty years. Ad agencies were able to attract the best and the brightest college graduates to work in their creative departments during this period, and it was often remarked that the advertising was better than the programming.

But with the advent of new technologies, like the Internet, mobile devices, social networks, and Twitter, marketers started to gradually worry more about the delivery vehicle than what was being delivered. The truck became more important than the cargo.

Nevertheless, the Unbreakable Rule about creativity still applies, no matter what technology is delivering it. A dull message coming to you on your Facebook page is going to get just as ignored as junk mail in your mailbox. It's the creativity behind the message itself, not the delivery method, that gets through. Dull arrows bounce off.

HOW CREATIVITY WORKS

Creativity is one of those elusive qualities that are hard to define. We all know when something's creative, mostly because it attracts our attention. It's new. But we don't know the precise features that make it creative. We just recognize when it is.

But that's precisely the point: Anything is creative when it's unexpected, or has never been seen before (at least by this generation). Human beings are programmed to respond to new stimuli. If we experience the same thing over and over we soon become habituated to it, and it fails to register. How often, for instance, do we drive the same route to work every day without thinking about it? But if the route changes because of a detour, the details stand out.

We almost have a sixth sense for creativity. This is why, when scanning through commercials, we can uncannily detect an entertaining spot even at 200 frames per second; enough to slow down and go back.

Creativity has this powerful allure we can't resist. It can come in many flavors but its one, common effect is on our emotions. When we are put into an emotional state, we are more open to suggestion. An emotional state increases our awareness, it makes our capillaries dilate, sensitizes our receptors, stimulates our synaptic response in the superior hypolingual-ya-ya, and all of that neuropsych mumbo jumbo. But that's not important. What's important is that when we are in an emotional state, we are in the complete power of whoever put us into it. They have our attention.

One creative technique to stimulate an emotional response is humor. Of all creative techniques, comedy is probably the most widely used, precisely because it is so powerful. A funny ad makes people laugh. Laughter is an emotional response. Laughter makes people feel good. It disarms. It makes people want to like you, want to listen to you, and want to do business with you. Make somebody laugh and you have them right where you want them.

Humor works best when it is unexpected. Old Spice, a dry old brand from the Age of the Dinosaurs came at us unexpectedly with a humorous campaign in 2009. No one had ever associated Old Spice, the aftershave your grandfather liked to use, with something hip and funny. Geico's humorous campaigns have also broken through because people don't expect an insurance company to be funny. People say, "Did you see that?" And they actually now go online to see if they can find the ad on YouTube and send the link to their friends. You could never make a message go viral like that if it was dull. But it is that creativity, especially the humor, that creates the viral effect.

Creativity has another psychological effect. It communicates the idea that your brand is smart. Creative people are inherently more attractive than dullards. Sorry to say, but it's true (at least it's perceived to be true and that's the same thing; see Rule #2). Creative people are perceived to be smarter. They're more fun to be around. They have something everyone envies, something that everyone hopes will rub off on them.

The same goes for companies. A company whose products are perceived as creative is one that is more attractive to people. This is part of Apple's appeal. Apple comes across in all of its marketing, from its ads to the design of its products, even to the black-shirted staff in its retail stores, as a creative, hip company. Apple's customers feel that hipness rubbing off on them. Even having just one Apple product, like iTunes, on their PC, makes them feel cool.

This effect of contagious hipness starts working even before a customer buys a product. An ad is frequently the first impression a consumer has of a company, so if the ad itself is creative, the conclusion flows to the impression of the company and its products. Instead of guilt by association, it's virtue by association.

On the other hand, if your marketing messages are dry and tedious, people are going to think the same thing about your product, however wonderfully it may test in your labs. By extension, they're also going to think the same thing about your entire company. This will hurt your ability to attract not just customers, but even talent and investors. It may not be fair, but fortune favors the cool.

MATCH CREATIVITY TO THE PRODUCT

While humor is a powerful, creative tool in persuasive marketing, creativity doesn't necessarily mean you always have to be the Class Clown of Commerce. Many products just don't lend themselves to humor (though we once created a highly effective, humorous TV campaign for Forest Lawn Mortuaries that resulted in dramatic sales—and not by killing people with laughter, as you were about to say). But creativity can also mean sparking any emotional response.

Hunger is another emotional response, probably the most primitive one there is. A restaurant that makes you hungry with mouth-watering close-ups of its food is actually being creative by making your stomach growl. A shampoo brand that makes you go ga-ga over an adorable baby is touching another emotion in you: the nurture response. Even an ad that arouses you erotically is using creativity. Anything that evokes an emotional response is itself a creative technique. We'll cover this principle in greater detail under Rule #7, Emotions Rule the World.

To achieve that emotional response, you need to match the creative approach to the product. You would never, for instance, try to win over customers to your cologne by showing charts and figures demonstrating the chemical superiority of your product over your competitors' (unless, that incongruity makes it funny, of course). Fashion and cosmetics are obvious cases for creativity. But even if your product is as dry as a tri-axially auto-stabilized dihedral wave induction chamber (whatever that is) for use in the aerospace industry, you should be creative in how you approach the engineers who you want to buy it. Remember, they are people, too. And though they may deny it, they are susceptible to being moved.

Just make sure your creative solutions are relevant to the product. A funny commercial may go viral, but if the comedy doesn't help your audience remember your product, or its benefit to them, it's just gratuitous humor. The last thing you want to hear is someone describing your hilarious commercial and not being able to remember who it was for, or what the point was.

Make sure your creativity is relevant to your core message.

THE COMPANY THAT SHREDS TORPEDOES

As an example of relevant creativity, take SSI Shredding Systems, a company that makes industrial-sized shredders. These are not the cute little paper shredders you use in your office to take care of incriminating evidence before the Feds arrive; these are gigantic, mechanical tyrannosaurs that eat entire cars like Cheetos. You'd think the no-nonsense, heavy-industrial nature of SSI would not lend itself to a creative marketing solution. But you'd be wrong.

During the discovery phase of our marketing project with SSI we noticed two things. The first was that whenever a sales person would talk to a potential customer on the phone, the first question they'd ask was never, "What kind of a shredder do you need?" It was always, "What needs shredding?" Each shredder was, essentially, custom built for whatever it was intended to shred. The founder of the company claimed that he could build a shredder that could chew up anything, anywhere, anytime. For instance, he boasted that once the Navy contracted him to shred its arsenal of obsolete torpedoes. His personal philosophy was that if the thing existed in the physical world, he'd figure out a way to turn it into itty-bitty pieces.

So "What needs shredding?" became the natural brand position of SSI. It was an expression of benefit to the customer's needs and, at the same time, a confident claim of superiority.

The second thing our marketing team discovered about SSI was how fascinating—hypnotic, really—it was to watch something being shredded. Standing over one of these giant machines, watching an entire refrigerator being chewed up like a Godzilla-sized graham cracker, made us cry out, "Again! Do another one!"

It was absolutely primal entertainment.

It so happened that the company had an archive of over twenty years' worth of videos of all manner of things being chewed up and spit out. SSI was always trying to push the envelope in what could be shredded and had a tradition of recording its achievements on video. There were hundreds of these videos on file; mattresses, computers, engine blocks, plastic bottles, refrigerators, titanium scrap (which sparks spectacularly when cut), even sports equipment, all being torn apart in the teeth of these huge, mechanical monsters. You could watch these videos for hours and not ever get bored.

Our idea was to take this treasure trove of destructive entertainment and put it up on the SSI website, and then to send out links to all of their customers under a marketing campaign we called "Watch it Shred."

In its print ad campaign, while all of its competitors were running ads showing pictures of their machinery, SSI's ads stopped readers with unexpected images, like a stack of old mattresses or Twinkies or bowling balls. The creative power of all the trade ads came from the idea of weird things being ripped to shreds. The implication being that here was a company that was not daunted by anything. The message was the challenge, "What needs shredding?"

The "Watch it Shred" campaign was dramatically successful. Within a month, the videos and the SSI site went viral. From an average of mere hundreds of visits a month, the company's site was suddenly getting half-a-million. This rate grew for months. As a result of all the interest in things being chewed to pieces, the SSI site was featured on the G4 gaming channel's segment of coolest websites. The History Channel's *Modern Marvels* series called the company to do a segment about SSI on their episode, "World's Sharpest." And David Letterman's producer called to have the company shred an entire car for the show. No problem. SSI ate entire cars for breakfast.

All very nice. But there were those at SSI who weren't impressed. What did all of this have to do with selling shredders? The problem initially was that the vast majority of the hits to the site were coming from people who hadn't the least interest in buying an industrial shredder. Millions of non-customers were flocking to watch stuff get pulverized. It was very cool—to teenage boys, maybe. But SSI wasn't selling 60 ton industrial shredders to teenagers—their dads, perhaps, but only if they happened to own a recycling company. This initial spike in visibility was all well and good, but seemed to be entirely to the wrong market.

All true, but within a very short time, an organic Google

search for "industrial shredders" brought the company—which had previously been in Search Engine Siberia somewhere after page six—up to the very top of the first page…without even paying for it. SSI kept this pole position from thereafter. This meant that an actual, potential customer, when searching for "industrial shredders", was most likely to see SSI first.

Qualified leads tripled. And sales more than doubled. For years the company's sales were fairly constant. But within the first year the company enjoyed a 250% jump in sales and has been able to sustain that volume, even through the Great Recession.

The marketing technique we used was to match the creativity to the product with a natural attractor, people's inherent fascination with destruction. This raised the overall awareness by generating momentum. As it turned out, all of those millions of teenage boys flocking to the SSI site to watch a Volkswagen being torn apart, towed in their Googly wake hundreds of qualified leads—each one in the market for hundreds of thousands of dollars of industrial equipment.

Even the generic search phrase "shredder" brought SSI up with several returns on page one, mostly because of the high volume of activity generated by people going there to watch things like bowling balls being pulverized. The company, which had previously been down in the weeds with a dozen other shredding competitors, now rose to the top, becoming, almost overnight, the number one industrial shredding company in the world.

The secret to this campaign wasn't simply a deft use

of online and trade media. It was the creativity of finding something that was inherently fun about the product itself. During the "Watch it Shred" campaign there was no hard sell of products or shredder models; it was all soft-sell, giving the viewer the gift of entertainment. But the entertainment was uniquely appropriate to the product and the primary customer benefit. The buyer of an industrial shredder was led to conclude, if an SSI shredder can do that to a torpedo, think what it could do my yard full of scrap metal.

YOU WANT YOUR MESSAGE TO GO VIRAL? BE CREATIVE

The crack cocaine of advertising now is viral marketing. YouTube has made it possible to put your TV spot up online and see it multiply your media like a virus. Everyone wants to do this; it's free, and you can reach millions of people. How can paying $2.6 million for a Super Bowl commercial compete with that? Well, one reason an advertiser might want to spend $2.6 million for a TV spot on the Super Bowl is so it *will* go viral. It's like an ad for the ad. You thought that ad was funny? Go online to see it again. And send it to all of your friends. Creativity actually multiplies that Super Bowl investment.

Take the famous Apple "1984"commercial, produced by creative agency Chiat Day a quarter century ago. It is still hailed as the greatest commercial of all time by most ad historians and critics. The spot, announcing the introduction of the first Macintosh personal computer, is a take on George Orwell's *1984,* in which a totalitarian corporate state (a thinly disguised IBM) is challenged by a revolutionary young woman who hurls a sledge hammer at the Jumbotron face of Big Brother. As the image of the dictator explodes in a blaze of light, the announcer says, "On January 24th, Apple will introduce Macintosh. And you'll see why 1984 won't be like '1984.'"

The commercial aired once—during the Super Bowl, of course. And yet, even before the Internet, it went viral, being played again and again on television as an example of creative advertising. To this day, it can be seen online, one upload of it boasting over 6 million views—this for a product that became obsolete before most of today's viewers were even born. That's viral.

You want your message to go viral? Make it creative. No one's going to upload a boring spot. Even if you do it yourself, uploading it to YouTube or Google Video, no one will pass it around unless it entertains.

Funny ads, of course, are easiest to make viral. Stick a sneezing panda in your commercial and you have a chance (unless, of course, that joke is already old). But it's not just comedic commercials that go viral; any highly creative, moving idea can do it.

In 2010 the Sussex Safer Roads Partnership, in the county of Sussex, England, posted a local public service announcement encouraging people to wear their seatbelts. The video is a highly stylized mime of a man sitting in a chair in his living room, pretending to drive. He smiles at his wife and daughter sitting on the couch, who smile back. Suddenly (in slow motion "suddenly"), he looks in horror as he sees that he's about to crash. His family rushes (in slow motion "rush") to his side and throw their arms around him in just the way a seat belt would restrain him. He crashes and everything in the room is hurled violently forward, except for him, saved by the arms of his family. A title comes up that says simply, "Embrace Life. Always wear your seat belt." Very simple, very creative, very emotional.

Even though the entire population of Sussex is about a million-and-a-half, over ten times this number have viewed the spot on YouTube since it was first uploaded. An estimated one million people viewed it within the first month of its posting and over 12 million saw it around the world within the first year. It was ranked as the number one YouTube video of all time for educational content.

So here we had a boring message, "wear your seat belt," presented in a very creative and emotional way. The production, though professional, was relatively inexpensive by industry standards (less than $100,000). It never aired on television and yet, to date, almost 14.5 million people have seen it and passed it forward to their friends around the world. Could this have been done if creativity had not been used? Would an earnest spokesman simply urging you to buckle your seatbelt have gone viral? Not unless they were naked. Or there was a sneezing panda. The very mechanism of viral marketing is driven by creativity. If your message is not creative, it will die.

AN EXPERIMENT YOU CAN DO IN THE PRIVACY OF YOUR OWN HOME

Marketers are so funny. They all have their favorite TV commercials. They, like everybody else, watch the Super Bowl "mostly for the ads." They like to be entertained. They can describe in scene-by-scene detail a funny commercial they saw. And yet, when it comes to marketing their own brands, they tend to lose their sense of humor. They seem to think, it's one thing for Geico or Budweiser to make them laugh and remember their brands; it's quite another thing when it's their own brand. Then, suddenly, they have this compulsion to bore everybody with a long list of features and benefits, as if nobody is going to scan right through it.

If you're marketing your own business, try an experiment with yourself: Watch your favorite TV show and note how many commercials there are (resist the overwhelming urge to scan through them if you've recorded the show). Note your reaction to the dull ones and to the ones you think are most entertaining. Then, in your imagination, replace the brands in them with your own brand. If you are bored by an ad, the chances are pretty good that everyone else will be, too. If an ad entertains you, it will probably entertain others.

Pay attention to your reaction to other marketing messages, not just commercials and ads. They are all around you. Even in residential neighborhoods, as we've already noted in an earlier self-experiment, these include yard signs, bumper stickers, logos on sweatshirts, bus posters, reader boards on the local churches, curbside characters dressed up like a slice of pizza or the Statue of Liberty. These things are all around you and yet you probably filter them out as part of the general clutter and environmental pollution. If you stopped to read and pay attention to every one, you'd go insane (or be insane). Now imagine your own company's message among all of those. What makes you think anyone but you will notice it? How can you compete with a dancing pizza?

This is why you have to be creative; to break through the clutter. If you aren't creative, you'll just sink into the weeds and die. When you're afraid to be creative, it will only show you are driven by fear, and nobody wants to hang around somebody who's afraid.

THERE IS NO FORMULA FOR CREATIVITY

This may surprise you. You may have encountered marketing companies who claim to have a scientifically proven formula for creativity—or who scoff at the notion of creativity entirely, claiming they have proof that a phone number repeated at least 14 times within a sixty second spot "works".

They lie.

Well, "lie" may be too strong. They're mistaken. Their reality is based on meticulously amassed data. And data and creativity, like drugs and alcohol, should never be mixed.

Years ago we worked on the advertising campaign for an internationally famous brand of cat food. In developing the scripts and storyboards for the TV commercials, we were given a specific formula by the client's team of brand managers. Marketing research had shown that if the cat (always a white Persian) licked its chops more than two times in the commercial, sales went down. If it licked only once, sales also went down. Two shall be the number of its licking. No more. No less.

We at the ad agency looked at each other with amusement, but the brand managers were not kidding. Wait, it gets sillier. Another element to the "proven" creative formula involved dinging a crystal goblet twice with a silver spoon; a signal to the Persian cat that dinner was ready. We were told that while we could photograph the dinging spoon in any way we wished, the dish had to be the same, the spoon had to be the same…oh, and the lighting had to be the same. Otherwise, we could get as "creative" as we wanted to with it. Any variation from this formula had been demonstrated to have catastrophic results in sales. Their "proof" had been that two years before, they'd allowed a director to ding the dish three times and sales went down that year.

We call this the "lucky socks" theory of marketing. Baseball players, being notoriously superstitious, have been known to credit a hitting streak to wearing a pair of "lucky" socks. Because they hit three home runs in a row while wearing those socks, they've concluded that it must have been the socks that were responsible for their streak, not any of the thousand other factors (such as batting skill, the pitcher, the distance to the fence, or the fact that they didn't get drunk the night before). Nope, it was the socks (see Rule #2, Perception is Reality). So don't wash those socks. The same phenomenon happens a lot in marketing. With all of the thousand factors that can influence sales of a product, like the state of the economy, new competition, or sunspots, seemingly rational marketers can think it's how many times a cat licks its chops that will make the difference.

So be wary of marketing companies that claim you don't need creativity, just their formula. There is no formula. Creativity is an art, not a science. In fact, the very act of trying to formulate creativity can work against its attractive power. This may seem to fly in the face of Rule #1, Consistency Beats Ability, but it doesn't really. The consistency that's important here is to keep developing creative ways to present a consistent message, so the message stays fresh, but consistent.

Creativity isn't easy. Even those of us who have made a pretty decent living as creative professionals don't always know how we do it. We just know that it comes out of countless hours of hard work, experience, and trying things that don't work. We've won Clios and Webbys, been published in industry annuals, seen sales go through the roof after creative campaigns, and generally kicked butt. But we're still not really sure where it comes from. We can't recall what we were doing when the idea came to us. We didn't put ourselves into a special, creative trance. We weren't wearing any particular pair of socks. The idea just seemed to come out of nowhere. We just knew it would work.

Hal Riney, one of the great creative admen of the twentieth century, said, "The frightening and most difficult thing about what some people call a creative person is that you have no idea where your thoughts come from. And you have no idea where they're going to come from tomorrow."

IT DOESN'T MATTER WHAT COLOR IT IS

How do you know if something's creative? It has nothing to do with how well it's designed, what color it is, what typeface you use, or any of those things your graphic designer is so passionate about. You could have a rigid corporate identity manual that mandates that you only use PMS Reflex Blue in all of your communications, and set your type in only Helvetica or Times Roman fonts (12/14, of course) and still be creative. A message is creative when it moves you. And it's not the type or the color or the pleasing use of white space that do that; it's the idea.

Of course, not to belittle the important work of graphic designers, or of the quality of every detail of your marketing communications, including the consistently refined typography and a pleasing application of color theory, but don't let that be a substitute for real creative thinking.

People aren't going to stop their DVR and back up to check out that commercial with the great typography. They're not going to remember that magazine ad with the rich use of white space. No one is going to click through an online banner just because it has an animated dancing baby. And people aren't going to search on YouTube for a commercial with pleasing color. People will only pay attention if what you say moves them with a creative idea. It's the content, not the form.

Without the idea, all of those so-called creative attributes are just meaningless decoration. But when they're associated with an idea, the consistent use of color, typography, design, imagery, all remind people of why they like you. It isn't the green and black logo of the mermaid that is the source of Starbuck's success. If that were true then all you'd have to do is use green and black on all of your own marketing materials and people would come like zombies to buy your products. But those arbitrary corporate colors, through consistent and creative marketing of the idea of Starbucks, have come to stand for the emotionally positive experience that customers associate with that brand.

The creativity is in the idea. It's the idea that moves you.

But the ultimate reason your marketing has to be creative is that it simply gets you more business. Unless you have unlimited media dollars and can afford to flood all channels with your message, you need to be creative to get noticed. As we've demonstrated, people are really good at filtering out the noise of the marketing wind. It's the same skill that a mother uses when, while chatting with a friend on a bench at the playground, she can pick out the sound of her child's cry of pain from all the cacophony of yelling children.

So simply increasing the volume—the reach and frequency in media terms—is not going to guarantee that your message and brand are noticed. If your message is dull, it can take hundreds of millions of dollars and billions of impressions to even be noticed. When your media dollars are limited, you don't have liberty to be boring. You have to be creative to break through. But even if your budget is not the issue, it's still just good business to make your marketing dollars go further by being creative.

SEIZE THE FUNNY BONE

Years ago we won a new advertising account for a local sports and auto retail chain called G.I. Joe's. We were told at the outset that, because we were in the midst of an economic recession, they could spend no more money on media. But could we help them with their message?

G.I. Joe's, which had started in the Pacific Northwest as an Army/Navy surplus outlet after WWII, sold sports equipment and auto supplies; things you'd do on the weekend. Their customer pool was overwhelmingly male, though there was a sizable female component, especially in the ski and exercise equipment areas. It occurred to us that people went to G.I. Joe's looking for help with their weekends; skiing, basketball, camping, hunting, fishing, and just working on the car. It was a place to help them escape.

This was the creative inspiration for the "Seize the Weekend" campaign. It was a call to action for people to make the most of their time off, and G.I. Joe's was the place to outfit them for that. The campaign used humor; guy humor. The spokesman, Merle Kessler, was an NPR comedian known for his fast-talking style. TV and radio scripts were written as one guy to another, with lots of macho empathy. As before, the commercials were still flogging items like Prestone antifreeze, Coleman lanterns, and Head skis, just like all sports and auto retail advertising. But the difference was the humor, much of it satirical. One spot made fun of a contemporary Calvin Klein Obsession commercial; but instead of beautiful models, it featured a middle-aged, bald man obsessing over his Coleman cooler and Valvoline motor oil (79¢ a quart, this week only!).

G.I. Joe's kept this humor up, producing over 80 funny commercials during the first year. The results were a 20% increase in sales. Before the campaign launched, the retailer had measured unaided brand awareness for G.I. Joe's (where marketing research asked the question, "Can you think of a sports and auto store?") and found it to be barely 6%. In other words, G.I. Joe's was almost invisible. After six months running the humorous Seize the Weekend campaign, the unaided brand awareness was again measured and it had jumped to almost 70%.

This campaign turned out to be an ideal demonstration of the power of creativity. G.I. Joe's had not increased its media buy; it had only changed the content of its ads. Where the old commercials had been dry and informative, they were now entertaining (yet still managing to get across the product information and sale prices). This converted into a dramatic rise in sales and a startling increase in G.I. Joe's overall brand awareness—a pretty good bonus for a campaign that wasn't supposed to be a "brand campaign." It also occurred during an economic recession, where you'd expect retail sales for things like recreation to take a dive, not actually go up.

Creativity was worth every penny.

During the late 1980s there was a study done at the London School of Economics that showed that ads that were categorized as "creative" scored six times better in terms of response and memorability than ads which were described as merely informational. We assumed by the latter that they meant the "an important announcement about your car insurance" variety. Whatever criteria the study used to define "creative" advertising, it was a powerful validation of the intuitive knowledge that you can attract more flies with honey. Six times more flies, as it turns out.

>DO THIS

Use creativity in your marketing.
Or turn out the lights and go home.

THE MEDIUM IS NOT THE MESSAGE

ARE YOU PREPARED TO DIE TO MARKET YOUR MESSAGE?

In 2010 a small street vendor in Tunisia, Mohamed Bouazizi, at the end of his rope, his tiny little vegetable cart confiscated by a corrupt police force, humiliated by government thugs, and with nothing to lose, decided to use the ultimate expression of protest to a brutal dictatorship that wasn't even letting a humble street vendor scratch out a living. He killed himself. And he did it in a theatrical and grizzly fashion; he set fire to himself—right in front of a government building for maximum visibility.

The act served to spark a massive revolution, not just in tiny Tunisia, but within weeks in Egypt, Libya, Yemen, Bahrain, Syria, all across the Middle East, and eventually across the world in a populist movement called The Arab Spring. People were fed up with being oppressed by their bully-boy dictators. The poor, desperate vegetable salesman did something that few people had the courage to do. With spectacular results.

Bouazizi's medium was his own life, combined with the horrible way he took it and the place he took it. But it was his message that sparked the revolution. If he had been just another depressed person ending his life, the manner in which he did it would not matter, and it would not have mattered why he did it. It was the message that made the gesture so powerful; made all the more so by the medium in which it was delivered.

In 1964 Marshall McLuhan, that great, one-man aphorism factory, wrote a book called *Understanding Media; The Extensions of Man*, in which one of his contentions was that the delivery vehicle of a message, the medium, was more important than the message itself. In other words, the truck was more important than its cargo. Few books, except maybe the Bible, have been more misread or misquoted than Marshall McLuhan's. It is certainly not the intention of this book to correct that. As far as we're concerned, McLuhan was asking to be misunderstood. He himself said that the medium was more important than the message, so there. It is ironic that, thirty years after his death, McLuhan's most famous idea, "the medium is the message," is itself more remembered than the medium in which it was first published; a paper book, set in moveable metal type.

But he was right in that people today have a tendency to worship the medium more than the significance of the message itself. The invention of writing, that leading-edge medium of over 5,000 years ago, probably thrilled the users of it far more than what was being written. Other than

The Epic of Gilgamesh, about all we have of the literature of ancient Sumer are inventory lists and tedious press releases lying about the wonderful deeds of the CEOs of Mesopotamia, Inc. *The Epic of Gilgamesh* itself isn't that great a read, if you want to know the truth, and the only reason anyone reads it at all is that it's required in many high schools as the first known work of literature. But we look upon those ancient scratches with reverence. Even the more ancient cave paintings of Paleolithic people are contemplated with awe, yet all they seem to be telling us is that these people liked to eat meat. A lot of meat. Not very profound there.

This adoration of media over message hasn't changed. People are more thrilled at Twitter than what's been twit (or tweeted, what *is* the past tense of that verb?) Being able to access the Web on a mobile device is more exciting than the ideas that can be accessed, or even if you can actually read it without a pocket magnifier. Much has been made of the phenomenon that the recent popular uprisings in Iran, Tunisia, Egypt and elsewhere happened on Facebook, as if people could never revolt before. Facebook was the story, not the self-determination of people throwing off their tyrannical overlords. So Time Magazine made Mark Zuckerberg its Person of the Year in 2010 for creating a website on which people could post messages and pictures of themselves. That some people used Facebook to communicate with other people in those revolutions was really no more significant than Paul Revere riding his horse through the Massachusetts night to tell colonists the British were coming. And when the Internet was shut down by the repressive regimes in the Middle East, the people connected through mobile texting. And when cellular services were restricted, they communicated through satellite phones, and eventually through just literal word of mouth. People with a huge idea find a way to spread it, regardless of the medium. The message finds its wings.

In the end, it isn't the medium that's remembered. It's the message. The message, in fact, becomes the medium.

Here's a personal example: Imagine two guys, Bert and Ernie, who are going to pop the question to their girlfriends... finally. Bert really goes all out with the medium. He hires a sky-ad company to pull a big banner behind a plane, he has a gourmet caterer prepare a magnificent picnic on the beach (let's assume it's a nice beach), he arranges for the two of them to be chauffeured to said nice beach in a stretch dune buggy, etc. In short, it's going to be the perfect moment, worthy of a reality TV show. Everything's going well when the big moment arrives. The plane pulling the banner flies by and Bert draws his beloved's attention to it. But there's nothing on the banner. It's just a plane towing a bed sheet. He has forgotten to write the proposal message for the sky-ad company to display. Everything is ruined. He's cranky. She thanks him for the nice picnic, a little disappointed, but his foul mood ruins everything. They don't get married. They break up, in fact. He does get his deposit on the sky ad back, though.

Ernie, on the other hand, is impulsive. While driving to the hardware store with his girlfriend, he simply blurts out,

"So, do you want to get married?" She does. They do. And both of them remember for the rest of their lives how he asked her on the way to the hardware store. The message, "Do you want to get married?" was the medium. Ernie could have asked it while they were reading the Sunday paper together, watching TV, barbecuing hamburgers, or brushing his teeth, and she still would have said yes, and they still would have remembered the circumstances of the moment because the message was what was important, not how it was asked.

The message, in other words, becomes the medium.

Two hundred years ago, two revolutions, the American and the French, were fomented using the 18th century mass medium of single-sheet newspapers. Every little town in the American colonies and France had a printing press, usually several. Printing presses existed all over Europe, in fact. They were the blogosphere of the 1700s. Every day revolutionary thinkers and pundits would write, publish, and circulate their papers up and down the eastern seaboard of North America, across the Atlantic, and throughout Europe as fast as horses and sailing ships could carry them. These broadsheets spread the word of revolution.

Nobody but history nerds remember that technical, media detail about those revolutions. What has been remembered about them is not these little newspapers; it was the ideas they broadcast. The ideas of democracy, individual freedom of expression, freedom of worship, and freedom from having soldiers quartered in your house (well, maybe not so much the latter), actually spread to other countries and started a mass wave of democratic revolutions in country after country for the next two-and-a-half centuries. Those ideas are still spreading. Whether the ideas spread by paper or the Internet or smart phones has been beside the point. It's been the messages themselves that created their own medium. A good idea finds a way.

A STRONG, CLEAR MESSAGE SENDS ITSELF

In the less lofty realm of commerce, this same marketing rule applies. The idea being circulated may be something as shallow as tangle-free hair conditioner instead of human freedom, but if the message is compelling enough, it will find its own way. The message is still the medium.

Fortunately we now live in a civilization where technology has made the reach of media more diverse and pervasive than ever. Messages can spread faster. Now your own audience itself can be your medium, propagating the message in the form of digital "word of mouth" (or "word of click"). A clever ad seen on TV can be posted on YouTube within minutes and spread to millions for free. A good idea, or a creative concept, goes viral quickly. But a dull message just sits there like bad milk at the back of the refrigerator, going bacterial. The only thing that gives a message even a prayer of going viral is if it's interesting, or funny, or both.

Of course most marketers think that their own messages are interesting. They believe that the simple statement of position, say that 15 minutes can save you 15% on your car insurance, is a fascinating concept and should automatically spread itself across the universe.

We've been asked by clients how we can help their messages go viral, as if there's a technological way to make sure that people will start passing them around the Internet, or at least make their computers do it while they're asleep. Of course there are technological ways. Most of them just backfire by pissing off your audience, so your future messages just get automatically dumped in the Junk Folder... or blocked altogether.

But one sure way to make something go viral—if you can call anything sure—is by making your message entertaining. Funny messages propagate faster and farther, which should be no surprise, but even intriguing messages, or messages that touch people's hearts, can also get picked up and passed on. The rapidly expanding viral campaign that boosted the Old Spice brand would have gone nowhere had not the ads themselves been funny.

Another sure way of making something contagious is to make it provocative, emotional, and easy to remember. The "Embrace Life" seat belt campaign went viral by being so creatively poignant. Bouazizi's message on the steps of that Tunisian government building was about as provocative as you can get. And it was easy to remember: "Let us go free!"

DON'T PUT ALL OF YOUR EGO IN ONE BASKET

Now all this may just sound like a cranky reaction to the fast pace of media technology that is sweeping across the planet. Entire new species of ad agencies dedicated to specific channels have popped up in the last ten years. There are agencies specializing in internet marketing (also called digital or digital-direct), mobile-only, SEO (search engine optimization), and viral-only, all promising the one answer to all of your marketing needs. But there is no one, perfect channel. You still need to make the right choices and a mix of media to get your message out.

Many of you may not remember how e-mail in the early 1990s was predicted to sweep away all other forms of communication. And long before that, broadcast TV was going to make radio a thing of the past. And almost a century ago, radio was going to do away with print. But all new media just gets layered into the lasagna. Today there may be more media choices than ever before, but they're still all in there. And each has its place.

But beware of single-media solutions. Just as there isn't one perfect food, you need a balanced diet.

There is a lot of hype about how social networking and SEO marketing are going to transform the way we all do marketing. Some marketing pundits have gone as far as proclaiming that these will replace all forms of marketing. Why would you need to spend money on advertising, for instance, if people needing your product or service can just find it by typing it into a Google search field? (What was your product or service, by the way?)

The trouble with SEO marketing is that, as a medium, it's severely passive and backward looking. This may sound like an odd thing to say about a rapidly evolving technology. It can be very useful in narrowing down leads for qualification, but it's only a tiny part of how a comprehensive marketing strategy should work. SEO faces the past, looking at historical behavior or past awareness of a product. There is yet no algorithm on Earth that can predict what you're going to be looking for in the future. If your business is a commodity—furnace repair, for instance—then a search-optimized website is probably good practice to make sure you're doing everything you can to draw customers in to repair their furnaces. This works for any well-established product or service.

But what if you have a brand new product? Or a service that's never been offered before? How are people going to search for something they don't even know exists? This is where traditional, integrated marketing practices come in. In order to get people to search for you, you'll have to somehow let them know you're there.

SEO by itself won't even help you float to the top in a crowded field. Experience with SSI showed that, after years in the business, they still couldn't turn up higher than page six on a Google search return for industrial shredders. It took something else, something creative, to really optimize it. It took an insight into human behavior that had nothing to do with conventional SEO techniques. They had to find something truly fascinating about industrial shredding that was going to attract millions of viewers to make it go viral, and to optimize the search engine in their favor. Videos of destruction, to be precise.

Then there's brand. If you have a strong brand, customers are more likely to search for you by name, in which case a strong SEO strategy is probably nice but not vital. If, on the other hand, you have an unknown brand, search optimization by itself won't help you there, either. Again, people won't even know to search for you. And if you're competing in a field with a strong brand, those guys will show up before you do. You may make the most technologically advanced running shoe in the world, but people searching for running shoes are still going to find Nike long before you. The strongest keyword, in short, is a well-known brand name.

Social network marketing is also a new hotness. The noble ideal behind it is that it simulates (or to proponents, facilitates) the kind of word of mouth endorsement that marketers have always believed is the strongest kind of advertising. If your father-in-law recommends a brand of pool filter, then it must be the best—unless, of course, you love him dearly but you don't think he knows jack about pool maintenance.

Social network marketing, too, depends on whether or not the people in the network want to share their likes. Just because you like a certain kind of music, it doesn't necessarily mean that all of your friends and family would like it too.

And even product affinity marketing has its limitations. Is the average person really going to set their profile to reveal that they always buy Tide detergent, or post on their wall, "Yippee! Just went to the supermarket and stocked up on Tide!"?

So the kinds of businesses that can benefit from social network marketing are limited. That being said, it's prudent to include a component of social network and search optimization into your overall media strategy. Don't just assume you can thrive on a limited diet of just those, though.

Concentrate on a strong, compelling message and spread it through a variety of channels.

MAKE THE MEDIUM AND THE MESSAGE ONE

It is possible, however, to use a medium itself to be part of the message. As Bouazizi, the poor, brave Tunisian street vendor demonstrated, a strong message combined with a riveting medium—in this case, suicide—can rock entire civilizations. His suicide sparked something in tens of thousands of sympathetic, equally frustrated Tunisians, and soon spread rapidly all over the Arab world, toppling some governments and shaking others to their core.

But the medium that Bouazizi happened to choose to convey his message, self-immolation in front of a government building, was just part of that message itself. If he had just held a placard in front of the building, or if he had even killed himself in the loneliness of his apartment with a drug overdose, it is doubtful that the revolt would have exploded. But it was the spectacular and horrific nature of his gesture, burning himself alive, that was critical to the power of the message. Fire was the medium. This act of violent self-destruction was itself, ironically, an extremely creative act. It changed minds. It changed behavior. It changed governments. It changed people's lives.

Of course the Web, Facebook, Twitter, and mobile texting all played their part in organizing and spreading the revolutions in Tunisia, Egypt, Libya, and elsewhere, but the original medium was the most primitive known to mankind: fire.

Bouazizi's story is terrible and heartbreaking. And it may seem crass to use him to illustrate a marketing principle. But he did not die in vain. He died heroically, trying to liberate his country. And his is an excellent example of the perfect integration of media and message. The media, in his case, were fire and his own death, the message was "We just want to be free."

Of course had Bouazizi chosen, out of whatever reasons thousands of people commit suicide, to kill himself in such spectacular fashion just because he was sad, and he had not connected his act of self-sacrifice to a powerful, emotional message, his would have been just another tragic death. Dying for a cause made his sacrifice meaningful. The medium he used made it stronger than if he had chosen a quieter, more "reasonable" medium than fire—which has to be one of the most painful ways to go. But doing it this way, by choosing this particular medium, he demonstrated his passion for the message.

Marketing, while seemingly trivial, is very serious business. It is fundamental to human commerce. Our very economy, our very livelihood depends on marketing. Bouazizi, humiliated and robbed of his last earthly capital and respect by the thugs of a dictatorship, was just trying to make a meager living selling fruit out of a wheelbarrow. He was engaged in business; marketing his products like Mark Zuckerberg markets his—only on a slightly smaller scale. Stripped of his little business and his last means of making a living, Bouazizi felt he had no other recourse. His last act of marketing was spectacular. Only he was no longer trying to market fruits and vegetables; he was marketing for freedom and had nothing left to lose (as Janis Joplin once sang). Both the medium he chose and the message he conveyed created a perfect storm, combined to achieve momentous social and political change. And they worked beautifully. It's just sad that the marketer couldn't have lived to see his success.

Admittedly, it's hard to see a connection between this story and case studies about body wash and beer advertising, not to mention a little tasteless. But in all of them are the same principle: Whether you're trying to start a revolution or just sell fruit from a cart, you need to consider the power of your message and the medium you use to deliver it. They have to support each other. And each has to be just right for the purpose. No one would burn himself to death in order to make the point that a beer is less filling. But he might do it to free his country.

The medium is not, as Marshall McLuhan contended, the message. The message can not only affect the medium itself, but can even find its own channel. When people are behind something they believe in, the word finds its own way to get out. But only if the message is strong enough.

>DO THIS

Create a strong message and
it will find its own wings.

UNBREAKABLE RULE #5

WORK HARD TO KEEP IT SIMPLE

SIMPLE IS BEST

The philosopher Samuel L. Jackson probably said it best: "I've had it with all these motherf*****' snakes on this motherf*****' plane!"

It is probably one of the most famous taglines for a movie, a movie with one of the best brand names ever, *Snakes on a Plane*. It says it all. It's emotional. It's evocative. It's memorable. It speaks directly to its target audience in language that demonstrates that here's a product that knows what they like, what they want, what they need. And most important, it says exactly what they're going to get; motherf*****' snakes on a motherf*****' plane. This isn't a movie in which the title is a metaphor of some underlying, universal truth about the human experience. It's not *The English Patient*. It's *Snakes on a Plane*. Brilliant.

Snakes on a Plane wasn't exactly *Harry Potter* in terms of box office success. It reportedly only made about double New Line Cinema's production investment of $30 million—which, still was a 100% return, not bad for a short term investment. And nobody was pretending it was *Citizen Kane*.

It is nonetheless a perfect demonstration of the Unbreakable Rule that governs a successful brand: simplicity.

Your customers have a powerful need for simplicity. Human beings are compulsively reductionist animals. We like simple concepts. They're easy to remember, easy to carry, easy to justify, and easy to act on. We're also lazy, or to put it more politically correctly, we're energy efficient. So if you make it too hard for us to figure out what you've got, we'll just go someplace else that won't demand so much of us.

Great brands are all simple. The brands and the brand positions they stand for may seem so obvious that few recognize how brilliant they really are. Coke, McDonald's, Volvo, Starbucks, Nike, Apple all represent simple ideas answering simple human needs. And the marketing messages that support those brands are, likewise, simple. They express ordinary, emotional human needs and values

Coke's message has always been familiarity, which equates emotionally to comfort. We're comfortable with things that we know. Coke's successive advertising taglines, "The Real Thing," "Coke is It," "Always," keep reinforcing that simple theme generation after generation. The same can be said for McDonald's, the world's most convenient food. Volvo has always stood for safety. Starbucks means community; it's today's village square where you can meet friends. Facebook stands for staying connected. And Apple has always made technology friendly to the majority of us who can't even use a remote control. These brands—and there are hundreds more—stand for simplicity itself.

CARL'S JR. = GLUTTONY

Here's an example of a brand that has reduced its message to the simplest—some may even argue—the most primitive terms. Carl's Jr., the fast-food chain, has been running the same campaign for years. Its ads feature young men cramming as much food into their mouths as possible. The message is about as simple a brand position as you're going to get: gluttony. The theme never wavers: Carl's Jr. is the place to go when you want to eat mass quantities. They know their market: teenage boys. These human pythons have to unhinge their jaws when they eat. They don't know restraint. And they also like to fantasize about having sex with people like Paris Hilton, Kim Kardashian, and Padma Lakshmi (also all featured prominently in Carl's Jr. advertising)—even though, if these kids keep eating like that, they're not likely to have sex with anyone. Older people look at these spots and wince. Young women look at these spots and wince. All those of us with fully developed pre-frontal cortexes can think of when we see a Carl's Jr. commercial is clogged arteries, coronary heart disease, Type II diabetes, colon cancer, impotence, and how life's going to catch up with these young men sooner or later. Probably sooner if they keep eating like that. All of us—except teenage boys—wince.

But Carl's Jr. is smart. They aren't having second thoughts about the simplicity of their message. And they aren't letting people outside their target audience influence their focus.

Since they started the gluttony campaign in the mid-nineties (in spite of the over-my-dead-body objections of soon-to-be-dead founder Carl Karcher) the chain's sales and growth have exploded, going from about 300 locations to over 1,000 today, including restaurants in places like Malaysia, Vietnam, Russia, and Poland. They've kept it simple, staying focused on their primary target market, young males.

Now we're not saying Carl's Jr.'s ads are models of aesthetic advertising. They offend a lot of people. We appreciate that there are forces in our society who would ban all fast-food advertising, just as Americans banned TV commercials for cigarettes in the 1960s. But these people are not the ones Carl's Jr. is talking to. Carl's Jr. doesn't care about pleasing people who wouldn't eat at their restaurants if they were starving to death, or even if they offered low fat salads (which they, in fact, do; you should try their Cranberry Apple Walnut Grilled Chicken Salad). Carl's Jr. knows who loves them, and they love them right back (see Rule #6, Give Love to Get Love). And they won't let themselves be distracted from their simple goal: Make teenage boys hungry for Carl's Jr.

IT'S COMPLICATED

But simplicity, like getting rid of a writhing mess of venomous reptiles on a plane, is not so simple.

Anyone charged with wrestling with a marketing strategy knows how easily a brand message can get away from you. Everyone in an organization—even the spouses of everyone in an organization—has an opinion about marketing. It takes a truly focused, strong personality, indeed, to stay the course and keep the primary message in focus.

We can sympathize: It's hard to stay on message. There are now so many more marketing channels than there were when Carl Karcher was flipping burgers in the 1950s. If you're a 21st century marketing director you have too many choices, and it's easy for you to get lost in the weeds as you contemplate how you're going to integrate your social networking strategy into your digital direct transaction platform while deploying your mobile device campaign. You've probably experienced the discomfort in meetings when some smart kid named Jasen asks questions like, "What is our Twitter strategy?" (He means, "tactic" not "strategy" but we won't nit-pick.) Everyone turns to you, about to click to the next PowerPoint slide, and you're supposed to have a ready answer. You feel tempted to just pull something out of the air to smack this smart-aleck down. Don't do it. Unless, of course, your next slide just happens to be about your "Twitter strategy", in which case… "Thanks for asking, Jasen."

This happens a lot. The process can easily be confused with the goal. The tactical choices can be overwhelming. And a weak marketing director can end up chasing after every new leaf that blows across the lawn. But the goal is not to take advantage of the next new thing in media, the goal is to get more people to drink Coke, drive Volvos, wear Nikes, meet at Starbucks, and unhinge their jaws for The Portobello Mushroom Six Dollar Burger™. Only at Carl's Jr.

So to Jasen's query (if you don't have a Twitter slide in

your deck) ask him right back how he sees Twitter getting to that ultimate goal.

How do you avoid getting lost in the weeds? The simple answer is just that: Keep it simple. It might actually help to have a big banner made and hang it over your marketing department, as a client of ours once did. The banner would proclaim what your brand position is; why it is that you're in business. Our client, SSI, the industrial shredder manufacturer, hung a banner over the entrance to their headquarters, asking in three foot letters, "What needs shredding?" It served to remind everyone coming to work, as well as every customer coming in for a factory tour, what the company was about. During the course of a workday, it can become easy to get side-tracked as you deal with problems. But at SSI, at least, you could look up and remind yourself that you were there to help your customers shred stuff. It's as simple as that.

Use any mnemonic trick that works for you and your team. Put the simple brand message at the top of every PowerPoint slide. Have a bronze desk plaque made. Print up buttons and pass them out. Require that all employees have the message tattooed on their foreheads (where legal). But, at a minimum, keep asking yourself and your team, how will this help us reach our goal?

IT'S OBVIOUS WHEN YOU DON'T KNOW WHAT YOU'RE DOING

A couple of years ago there was a great deal of comedy derived from a famous PowerPoint slide that the Pentagon was using to explain its strategy in Afghanistan. The unintended hilarity of the slide was that it looked like a flowchart spun by a spider on LSD. It was incomprehensible. Since no one, including and especially the architects of America's invasion of Afghanistan, seemed to be able to agree on what the strategic goals were (to get rid of the Taliban? to defeat Al Qaeda? to strike back for 9/11? to bring freedom and democracy to the Afghan people? to reopen the Silk Road to China?), the PowerPoint slide was a kind of MRI image of that organizational dysfunction, a cross-section of the institutional Alzheimer's syndrome that afflicts people who get down in the weeds. You didn't have to look at this slide but for a nano-second to get the real message: "We have no idea what we're doing."

General Stanley McChrystal, then commander of NATO forces in Afghanistan, said, with perfect comedic timing: "When we understand that slide, we'll have won the war." But, even as he brought down the House Committee with that great one-liner, he put his finger on it. The goal was to win the war. But the process was getting in the way of that. McChrystal later said, "It's dangerous because it can create the illusion of understanding and the illusion of control." And Marine Corps General James Mattis put it even blunter, "PowerPoint makes us stupid." The Marine Corps really knows how to keep it simple.

Historically, the campaign in Afghanistan is a beautiful demonstration of the danger to marketing campaigns which have no center. How many of us have tried to stay awake during presentations with slides no less complicated than the infamous Pentagon slide? Your overall impression is that the person making the presentation doesn't know what he's talking about. He's trying to make up for the fact that there's been no clear thinking by showing you how hard he's worked on this slide. If you want to be the smart ass at the boardroom table, just ask the question, "How is this going to help us win the war?"

Every marketing presentation should begin and end with the main goal, stated as simply as possible. Ideally that goal should be the header or footer of every subsequent slide so everyone is reminded of what we're trying to do here. But that's in an ideal world, where snakes are not allowed on planes.

Think of your marketing campaign like a military campaign. This is an analogy that has long been popular with marketing professionals, few of whom have ever actually been in a real war, but who love how macho it sounds. So when you are fighting a war, as every good military commander knows, the simplest plan has the best chance of success. The one thing that all of the great historical military catastrophes have in common, from Waterloo to the Little Big Horn to Vietnam, is that they were all the result of overly complicated plans, requiring too many things to go just right, diluting too many forces, and confusing the troops. The very same thing applies to marketing. The simplest marketing plan, with the simplest message, has the greatest chance of succeeding. Find your target, concentrate your artillery, and keep blasting away—until the target agrees to eat your burgers.

SIMPLE IS HARD

"I would have written a shorter letter, but I didn't have time." A famous line apparently first written by 17th century mathematician, Blaise Pascal. Ironically, many people, from Mark Twain to T.S. Eliot, have riffed on this quip in order to make it even shorter. But it is, nonetheless, a universal truth: Making something simple takes work.

The sad truth is that when your marketing messages get too complicated, the only message that comes through is that your company itself is too complicated. You might have spent thousands of consultant-hours and hundreds of thousands of dollars in market research crafting a marketing position that takes into account every stakeholder's opinion, every possible medium, every product feature, every focus group's input, and every bullet point in your mission statement, and the only thing you'll convey is, "We don't know what we're doing." People can smell that a mile away.

Ever notice when a politician is asked a direct, simple question by the press—say, "Are we going to war?"—and he doesn't answer it directly or simply, but starts nuancing the hell out of his answer? What are you thinking? "We're going to war!" Or ever notice your reaction to a direct marketing letter that takes paragraphs to get to the point, or how you feel when you open up the terms and conditions of your credit card agreement? Do you read it? Or do you think, they're hiding something?

But much of the time these people aren't being purposefully deceiving. They just haven't taken the time to simplify their message, to write a "shorter letter." Lawyers who compose terms and conditions for credit card companies aren't trying to make it simple for the average person to read; they're just trying to make sure every conceivable situation is covered to protect their client. It's hard enough to do that, much less attend to the brand perception of the bank. The irony is that all of those pages of fine print and prevaricating language directly affect the perception of the bank's brand, and not for the best.

Simplicity is itself part of the message. And it takes a lot of work.

THE TWITTER EXERCISE

Here's a simplicity exercise you can do: Take a wordy, famous piece of literature, like the Lord's Prayer, the preamble to the U.S. Constitution, or Hamlet, and reduce it to 140 characters or less. This is a fun game, but it's also useful to get into the habit of simplifying your message.

For example, here's a tweet version of the *Gettysburg Address*:

87 yrs ago: nu nation, all men=! Now civil war :(This hallowed ground. Dead not die in vain! Gr8 task b4 us. Gvt by&4 peeps not go away!

Not as elegant as Lincoln's gorgeous prose, but this is only an exercise in keeping it simple.

You can also take your own company's mission statement and see if you can reduce it to 140 characters or less. This may turn out to be even harder than Tweeting Hamlet's soliloquy on existentialism. You know, "To be or not to be…"

While we're not suggesting that you twitterize your advertising with ugly text abbreviations, the practice of paring messages down to their essence is a good one.

NIKE DOES IT

In 1988 the bosses of Nike honed their brand expression from "There is no finish line" to the simpler, "Just Do It." This simple phrase says everything it needs to about the philosophy of Nike. It means decisiveness, action, results. It means stop talking and start walking (or running). It provokes the customer who wants to lead a more active life. It also speaks to the corporate culture of Nike, where inventiveness, innovation, and entrepreneurship are rewarded. It even serves as a rallying cry for a whole generation of people to take charge of their own destinies. "Just Do It." is not just a slogan, it's a rule for living.

The Nike brand extends beyond the tagline. The mark itself, the Swoosh, is so simple it's become almost a universal icon for decisiveness and action. It can even be used without the brand name, Nike, for people to recognize it. Nike commercials, stylistic and inventive (obeying Rule #3, Be Creative or Die), all convey the "Just Do It" philosophy. They don't talk about shoe design or superior orthopedic engineering. They talk about being a superior human. Nike, in other words, is the brand of superior humans. Like you. Can't get any simpler.

So successful was this simplified branding that Nike went from 18% share of the athletic shoe market (behind arch-rival Reebok) in 1988 to 43% in 1998, and from about $877 million in annual sales to $9.2 billion during that same decade, and to almost $20 billion in 2009. The Nike brand position is now so strong that people will buy Nike products for the Swoosh alone, to demonstrate their inherent superiority, even though 80% of athletic shoes (what we used to disparagingly call "sneakers") are not used for athletics at all.

But Nike's success and brand dominance would not have happened, in spite of the inspired slogan and elegantly simple logo, if hundreds of marketing professionals at Nike and its ad agency, Wieden+Kennedy, had not worked their butts off making sure the brand stayed simple and did not start drifting over the years. This became even harder to do after Nike had become the number one athletic brand.

There is a temptation by each succeeding marketing director, and by each new ad agency, to put their own creative stamp on a brand—if not change it outright. But this temptation should be resisted if the brand is already strong and simple. Companies like Nike, GE, Toyota, McDonald's, and Coke work diligently to keep the essence of their brands simple, long after the original creators of their brands went on to the happy hunting ground.

Crafting a simple brand position is much harder than it looks. It takes a lot of work, tons of skill, and even more time to hone down the thing so that it looks easy. But behind every great, simple idea, there are countless years of sweat, experience, trial, error, discovery, and insight. It just looks easy at the end. Coke didn't suddenly become the global brand that can use the simple tagline "Always" and have people instantly know what that means. Coca Cola marketers worked for over a century on the brand position. They worked so hard that the very term "Coke" has come to stand for the entire category of soft drinks. People will say "Wanna go get a Coke?" even if they order a root beer.

While your highly paid army of IP lawyers strive to enforce the sanctity of your trademark, your marketing people secretly love it when people use your brand to stand for the whole category, like Coke, Kleenex, Google, Aspirin, iPad, and Sharpie. It means you dominate the field.

To be a great brand you have to stick to it. Don't get distracted. Stay focused, even if you're just a little guy. All the great brands were little guys once. Whenever you do a new ad campaign, keep asking yourself the question, "How will this support our main message?" You want people to be able to describe in a phrase what your company stands for. You want them to recognize your brand a mile away while they're moving at 80 miles per hour. You want them to think your message is so simple that they say, "I could've thought of that."

But they didn't. That's where the genius and work is. They didn't.

>DO THIS

Make your message simple. Now
make it simpler. Repeat as necessary.

UNBREAKABLE RULE #6

GIVE LOVE
TO GET LOVE

MUTUAL LOVE: THE NUCLEAR FORCE OF A BRAND

This is the part of the book where the group hug comes in. Don't cringe. Whether or not you want to admit it, when you're in marketing, you're in the love business. Regardless of what people want or need, if they have a choice between doing business with a company that loves them or one that just sees them as a revenue stream, they'll pick love. In fact, love will actually trump many other qualities, including and especially price. You can undercut your competition on price and you'll still lose. If you think you can win at that game, try selling a PC to a Mac owner. Mac owners love Apple. And Apple loves them.

Remember the Cola Wars from the 1980s? The deciding factor wasn't the scientifically proven quality in blind taste tests of Pepsi over Coke, it was the fact that Coke drinkers loved Coke. Period. And Volvo drivers love their Volvos because they come from a company that cares about their safety.

This goes to the essence of good branding: Love and you'll be loved back.

Building an emotional bond should be the goal of every successful brand (see Rule #7, Emotions Rule the World). No rational argument stands a chance against love. A brand promise based on lowest price is easily beaten by the next competitor who…well…beats your price. A brand that's known for being the biggest company is beaten by a brand that suddenly becomes bigger, in which case the previous "biggest" becomes the "loser" brand. But a brand that has an emotional connection with its customers—one that is beloved—is bound by one of the strongest forces in the known universe. This is why you can try to win over Mac owners with low price and the technical superiority claims of PCs versus Macs all day, and they'll still just look at you like a bemused True Believer and shake their heads in pity that you just don't get it. Of course Macs are more expensive, they'll admit. But they're worth it.

A strong emotional bond between a brand and its customers is so powerful that it can weather almost anything: upstart competitors, economic downturns, taste tests, price wars, even tainted meat scandals. About the only thing that can break that bond is a leveraged buyout by a company that chooses to dissolve the gobbled-up brand to the greater glory of its own corporate ego, as when Macy's chose to absorb venerable and beloved regional department stores like Meier & Frank, Hecht's, Robinsons, I. Magnin, Filene's, Jordan Marsh, and Bullocks.

If, heaven forbid, HP were to take over Apple, say, and

HP's management team was so moronic as to replace the Apple brand with its own (as it did with Compaq years ago), that would sever that almost fanatical loyalty of Mac owners and not only kill a strong brand, but kill all the steady business that went with it. It's probably not going to happen, but we're just using it as an example. Other companies, in taking over competitive companies, have made that mistake, so it's not unheard of.

LOVE HAS REASON THAT REASON DOESN'T KNOW

Customers who love you are loyal. They are much harder to woo away by competitors, even with good, scientific reasons. This principle is closely linked to Rule #4, Perception is Reality. People will love your brand far more than for the cold, measurable specs of your product. It's you they love. It's your company. It's your brand. Your fine products are just physical manifestations of that infatuation they have with just the idea of you. Starbucks isn't the most successful brand of beverage retailers because they have clinically proven better coffee (in fact, many coffee aficionados turn their noses up at those "bean burners"). They're successful because their customers love them, and they want them to succeed. Customers feel welcomed into their neighborhood Starbucks. The baristas remember their names and frequently their usual order. They see homemade little tributes to "customers of the month" on display. Even if you go into a Starbucks in a different city, you're greeted as though you are still a neighbor. They write your name on your cup as they take your order, making it just for you.

Starbucks, in short, knows how to seduce us. They had us at "hello."

Marketing studies—yes, with taste tests—have shown that people who have coffee prepared for them at a Starbucks swear that it actually tastes better than the same coffee they make for themselves at home with the same beans with the same equipment (bought at Starbucks). This is a peculiar phenomenon. It doesn't make any sense, unless you take into account that emotional bond. If you are a loyal Starbucks customer, you are emotionally ready to be pleased the moment you walk in. It isn't just the coffee. Hell, you could get that at work, probably from a Starbucks urn delivered by Starbucks. It's the feeling of treating yourself with a little micro-vacation. It's the way they make you feel even before you walk up to the counter.

This emotional bond works with any product. We have a friend who has an unshakeable loyalty to BMW. He has never owned another brand of car (at least since he's been able to afford it). When he bought a BMW that seemed to be in the shop more often than not, we teased him about it. His ready response was that when you have such an expensive, finely-engineered, road machine, you expect it to be temperamental. To those of us who just couldn't understand his seemingly blind infatuation, it seemed like when you spend $86,000 on a car, you should expect it to work. But we just didn't understand.

THE DISNEY EFFECT

Another company that is a master of this emotional

bonding is Disney, particularly Disney Theme Parks. Like anti-Starbucks partisans, people who don't like Disney just don't like it; you can't win them over by reason. They simply see corporate schmaltz in the service of overcharging their customers for a day of shallow entertainment. They insist the rides are demonstrably more thrilling at Six Flags (as measured by g-forces and barf bags). The food is better at Knott's Berry Farm. The value is greater at Universal Studios. You just can't sway those people. They are loyal to their own brands of amusement parks for their own reasons.

But regular Disney customers see it the opposite way. To them, it's not about price. In fact they are willing to pay more to go to the real thing, Disneyland, than to some feeble, wannabe park. They use the same cultish argument as do Mac owners about their more expensive Macs. It is about value, but the value is perceived far greater at Disney, in spite of its more expensive admission. Why is that?

It's because of how they feel before they ever go to Disneyland. The very brand name itself (though one of the most aggressively protected brands in the world) has become synonymous with warmth and love; someplace wholesome you can take your family—or your children on your court-mandated weekend with them. People go to Disneyland primed to feel good. It's "The Happiest Place on Earth," after all and, damn it, they're going to be happy if it kills them!

You'll find that it works. Even on hot days, when the lines are long and people have every reason to be cranky, there seems to be an aura of conviviality radiating from people.

People in those long lines are talkative, making fast friends with fellow tourists from all over the world. Everyone's in a good mood. Employees (or "cast members" as they're called) all seem genuinely cheerful and selflessly helpful. None of it feels forced or fake; they're either really good actors (cast members indeed) or are genuinely happy to be working there. We'll talk more later (under Rule #9, Everything is Marketing) about integrating your brand with your own employees, but an organization with a happy workforce is generally a sign that love is at work. And while Disney employees undoubtedly have their complaints, they don't show it to the public.

We've had long conversations with Disney "cast members" (some of our best friends, in fact, blah, blah, blah) and we have always been struck by how frank they seem. There is every reason, in the confidentiality of their personal, off-the-job talk, for them to let us know what they really think. But we've never heard them say anything really sinister about working for Disney. Most seem to genuinely love it. Anti-Disneyites (for whatever reasons) don't like to hear this. They think these people have been brainwashed. And, of course, they're right; all marketing is a form of brainwashing, but it doesn't mean that the pro-Disney faction is telling lies. Really effective brainwashing is based on perceived truth (Rule #2, Perception is Reality).

So people who visit Disneyland, people who work for Disney, and even people who are against the whole concept as fake and shallow, all have an emotional opinion. None of it is based on data. Disney Theme Parks are expensive.

Lines can sometimes be two hours long for two minutes of moderate, kinetic fun. The rides at Six Flags are indeed more terrifying. And a healthy hike on the Pacific Coast Trail is probably more spiritually uplifting (and terrifying if there are bears).

But Disney loyalists are loyal for life. They've often been coming to Disneyland for generations; it's part of their family tradition. They own all the Disney animated movies. Many own Disney stock. Their children, who have probably never seen an actual Mickey Mouse cartoon, know him and love him. Some have been waiting their entire lives to make the pilgrimage there. Indeed, it is almost a shrine to some.

We have friends who spent a vacation at Walt Disney World. Their seven-year-old daughter was looking forward to collecting autographs from all of the Princesses; Snow White, Cinderella, Pocahontas, Ariel, Aurora, Mulan, Belle, the whole gang. But at the end of the day, they never ran into Cinderella. Their little girl was distraught as they left the park. A Disney cast member asked her why she was crying and she said she never got to meet Cinderella. When they got back to their hotel room, there was a handwritten note on the little girl's pillow:

"Dear Allison, I am so sorry that I wasn't able to see you today. I hope you can come again because I really wanted to meet you. Love, Cinderella."

That's what we mean by giving love in your marketing. The Disney machine was so efficient and so caring that they spontaneously went out of their way to track this little girl down and give her the thing that would make her day. We dare say that she probably still has that note up above her bed, and will bring her own daughter to Disneyland some day.

Disney is an example of emotionally powerful marketing. The marketers there, beginning with Walt Disney himself, have consciously known how to exploit that bond, how to make it stronger, decade after decade. And the secret that Walt Disney understood and passed on—the secret to get people to love your company—is to love them first.

LOVE WORKS BOTH WAYS

John Lennon may have sung about it most famously in the song, The End, with the famous lyric: "And in the end the love you take is equal to the love you make" (though the actual couplet was supposed to have been written by Paul McCartney), but this is an ancient principle, a concept that is thousands of years old. It is the principle of absolutely selfless generosity. If you give love, you get love in return.

This just doesn't apply to spirituality, of course. We're not about to sneak in any New Age propaganda here (Ha! Just when you thought you'd bought another book about marketing!). It also applies, in the most blatant, materialistic, and crudest sense to marketing. It is the essence of the 6th Rule: Give Love to Get Love.

If you constantly show that you genuinely love your customers, your customers are more likely to love you back.

As we've already pointed out, anyone would prefer to do business with someone who loved them than with someone who was just trying to sell them something. No one likes the feeling of being sold to. Our defenses go up immediately, even if we want the thing, or need it. Most people appreciate the soft sell, at least on the receiving end.

And yet the myth of the hard sell seems more alive than ever. Current advertising is thick with it. Rarely does it respect you, or seem to appreciate that it just interrupted your entertainment. It breaks in on your favorite show and starts yelling at you about your blackheads, your erectile dysfunction, or how you haven't given serious thought to your retirement plan (you haven't, have you?). It is obvious that these companies don't love you. They just want your money. And, incredibly, they expect that you have so little self-possession that you'll sit there meekly and listen to their "important message about your auto insurance."

But think about the companies that entertain you with their commercials. They seem to appreciate that they've interrupted you, and by way of a peace offering to calm your irritation, they make you laugh. A funny commercial itself is a gesture of love and respect. These companies give you something for free; a little joke. And laughing out loud makes you suddenly feel good. You feel good about the company. You like them. You may actually sit through their commercial and (if it's crafted well enough) even remember their product.

This is why that study at the London School of Economics, showing that entertaining advertising did six times better than informational advertising, was no big surprise. We've all experienced this when we're the "targeted" customer. But when we're on the other end of the marketing, we just don't seem to apply it to our own customers.

In fact, the very notion in the marketing industry about "targeting" customers itself makes them seem like prey, not objects of affection. If we would offer any specific advice on how to change your emotional bond with your customers, stop calling them "target markets". Do you refer to your family as "targets"? Or your friends? Well, stop thinking about your customers that way.

YOU CAN'T JUST TALK ABOUT LOVE

But making funny ads isn't the end of it. You can't make an award-winning commercial for watery beer and expect your customers to order another round. Everything you do for your customers, from your advertising to your customer service to the actual products themselves, all has to be a gesture of love.

You have to genuinely love your customers to expect them to love you back. It can't be just talk. And that means going all out. You have to mean it. We can all smell rotten garbage through the air freshener. It's like a boyfriend who keeps saying "You know I love you, baby," but has a funny way of showing it by his abuse, neglect, or infidelity. Have you ever been out to dinner with someone who seems to be nice to you and is snotty to the waiter? We all recognize fake love when we see it.

If you're in business you have to create and nurture a company whose entire culture is based on love; love of your customers, love of your employees, love of your products and services, and even love of yourself. All of this has to be sincere. If love is absent anywhere in your organization, the whole thing starts to unravel (see also Rule #9, Everything is Marketing).

"What?" You're sputtering, "Why do I have to love my employees? I pay them to be nice to my customers. It's their job!"

But remember: To your customers, your employees are you. Your receptionist, your customer service people in India, the people on your factory floor, your managers—everyone is the face of your company. And if they're unhappy, that's the face your customer sees. Of course, you can't order them to "be happy or else", though we've known companies that have tried this, with severe backfire. And you can only hide abuse at your offshore factories for so long before the nasty truth gets out. Try to explain those suicide-prevention nets below the windows.

Most customers are themselves somebody's employee. They have far more empathy with your own employees than with your faceless brand. To your customer, your employee is your company's face. So you have to make sure those employees feel loved, so they love working for you. They have to be genuinely happy in their jobs or their customers will pick up on it, pitting both your customer and your employee against you. It's the Starbucks Effect. You want both your customer and your employee to love you.

Think of it like a marriage. As long as both people love each other, all the little frictions in their relationship—the clothes left on the bedroom floor, the forgetting of important anniversaries, the mess in the kitchen—are trumped by that love. But if love is not there, it's those very little frictions that become the flashpoint for a breakup. If your employees and customers don't love the idea of your company, they'll be looking for grounds for divorce with every little thing that irks them about you. But if they do love you, they'll be blind to your imperfections.

In North America, Nordstrom is the synonym for great customer service. Everyone knows this, even in parts of the world that don't have a Nordstrom store. Great customer service is the Nordstrom brand. And there are lots of testimonials passed around about Nordstrom's return policies; like the famous one about the old man in Alaska returning a set of bald tires, in spite of the fact that Nordstrom doesn't sell tires. But most people who shop there have experienced this customer service first hand, even though the average person would not try to return tires. Their belief in Nordstrom comes not from banners or ads proclaiming excellent customer service (which you never see in any of Nordstrom's communications), but from the employees themselves practicing actual customer service. Nordstrom walks the walk.

Even people who don't have a Nordstrom near them, or who have never shopped at one, know of anecdotes of customer service; items returned months later for a torn seam, items exchanged for more expensive replacements without extra charge, items returned without receipts, items returned that Nordstrom never carried. Many of the stories are myths, but following Rule #2, Perception is Reality, they are recounted and believed by customers to reinforce their own love of the Nordstrom brand.

Nordstrom's customer service policy empowers their employees to be creative in responding to complaints. Their corporate philosophy is founded on the idea that a complaint is actually a golden opportunity to win over a customer for life, in the way the complaint is resolved. So they give their employees freedom to do that. They know that losing money on a returned item is likely to result in future sales that will more than make up for it. Face it, would you be more likely to shop at a store that took back your pumps with a broken strap without question, or one that explained its complex return policy? Which one gets your love?

Contrast this Nordstrom experience with a common one at another retailer, a big box chain known for its low, low prices (who shall remain nameless because, aside from libel suits, we just don't think it's very loving to name names when there are faults): Frequently, waiting in line at the checkout in one of these stores, you'll overhear employees talking across their registers about the unfairness of working there. They talk trash about their supervisors. They complain about their hours. They gossip about fellow employees. And worse, they occasionally commiserate with each other about some idiot customer. (Not you. Of course, not you.) This store is known for its cranky clerks. But that's what you put up with for low, low prices.

But there is no love here. There is no love of management for the employees, or vice versa. And there is certainly no love for the customer, in spite of all the banners and ads bragging about their excellent customer service. These employees, these visible faces of the company, are ignoring you while they talk to each other. You're just another transaction before their much-needed break. Even as they bad-mouth other customers, it never occurs to them that you're offended inside, and that if it weren't for this eight dollar toaster oven, you'd get it at Nordstrom—if Nordstrom sold toaster ovens—even for nine dollars.

But even if it did occur to these unhappy employees that you were offended, it wouldn't matter because they don't feel any love for their company. They have no love to pass on. They don't care if you ever come back. It's just a shift job to them, at a barely living wage. And you can feel it and probably empathize.

Or there is this other common experience you may recognize: You notice in some of these big box retailers that in the checkout area there are twenty open registers, with never more than one or two people in any of them. But the customer service counter (where the returns happen) has just one, long line. Here's the brand message of this store: If you're buying something, we love you. But if you're returning something, please take a number.

Love is in deeds not words.

YOU CAN'T FAKE IT, EITHER

There are no shortcuts to loving your customers. You can't check it off by hiring an elderly person to greet them at the door, droning a flat script, "Welcome to Big Box, can I get you a basket?" You can't hang a banner that proclaims "We care," and think mission accomplished. You can't just stick a paragraph in the employee handbook, stating that the customer comes first.

If you can't show love to your employees, how are your customers supposed to believe you love them? You have to really, really love your customers. And in order to do that you have to love them through your surrogates, your employees. Which means you have to really love your employees; through your policies, their compensation, their benefits, your fairness, your respect for their needs. In short, you have to make sure they're happy. Crusty old-world managers like to say, through clenched cigar, "I'm not trying to win a popularity contest. I make them feel loved every two weeks in their paycheck." But that doesn't buy love, or loyalty, or job satisfaction. It only buys the bare minimum performance, and puts you in the role of The Boss. And not the Beloved Boss, either.

So make sure your employees are happy. Then, if your employees are happy, and love you back, it will show in their enthusiasm for their work. And they'll pass that love on to your customers, who become *their* customers, whom they will love in their own, innovative way. Appropriately, of course.

RECIPROCAL AFFINITY

Technically, in marketing jargon (which has to be one of the most jargon-rich professions outside of the Military Industrial Complex), this principle of giving love to get love is called Reciprocal Affinity. It makes it sound more technical. But it's a principle that's been a known virtue of good marketing for centuries. Walt Disney understood it. Starbucks understands it. So does McDonald's, Toyota, Volvo, Apple, FedEx, BMW, Nike, Nordstrom, and hundreds of other successful companies. Even companies whose lifeblood is not based on retail customer service, understand it. All businesses need to understand it and believe in it in their hearts and deeds.

Everyone involved with your company is part of Reciprocal Affinity.

Your product designers, motivated by their feeling of support and your appreciation for their genius, and by feeling like they're a part of a cause, will work nights and weekends to perfect and improve your product.

Your factory workers, who love working for your company because your company demonstrates its love and respect for them by your policies, benefits, compensation, and care for their well-being, will be extra diligent in assuring the quality of the products they send out the loading dock.

Your sales force, feeling your appreciation of their work, will be able to sell your product with sincerity, genuinely believing in it and genuinely believing in the company behind it; their company.

Finally, and first, you have to love what you do. Look at your product or service. You should love it so much that you want to marry it. You should love it so much that you'd do it as a hobby, even if you wouldn't make a cent on it. If you're selling carpet, you need to really love carpet. If you're making solar panels, you have to love the thing that makes your solar panels superior to any other. If you do love what you do, that will come through to your employees, to your sales force, to your vendors, and to your customers—everyone will love it, too. Love is contagious.

And in the end, when your customers unpack your lovingly made product and plug it in, they will love it and love you for making it for them. It's all part of the great circle of life. Or at least, the circle of commerce.

This is Reciprocal Affinity. You love me. I love you. Everything you do for me, from your entertaining commercials that seem to ask my pardon for the interruption, to your sincerely caring customer service, to the very design and reliability of your products...it all makes me love you right back.

BUT WHAT IF I'M NOT THE LOVEY-DOVEY TYPE?

Too bad. Make yourself love. Love isn't about how you feel, it's about what you do. If you want to thrive in this world, the truth is that you need other people. And you need those other people—your customers, your employees, your family, your constituents, your shareholders, your friends, even perfect strangers—to love you back.

This isn't a religious thing. Or a Flower-Power-Gandhi-philosophical thing. It's a practical truth. It's good business sense. And it's good social sense. It's how things get done. And how things move forward. People who love each other tend to become more accomplished because they realize we're all in this together. They work and fight for each other.

This doesn't mean you have to be sappy and sentimental about it. But it does mean you have to be conscious of how you treat everyone, not just your customers, and not just the people you may happen to be in actual love with at the time. Everybody.

As it turns out, love is the answer.

>DO THIS

Love your customers. Love your
employees. Love your products.
And the love will come back to you.

UNBREAKABLE RULE #7

EMOTIONS RULE THE WORLD

"I'VE FALLEN AND I CAN'T GET UP!"

In 2007 USA Today ranked this phrase as the most memorable ad slogan of the previous 25 years. After a quarter of a century, Life Alert Medical Alarm Service is still running essentially the same commercial (remade each year with an all new cast of amateur, senior citizen actors) featuring a re-enacted scenario in which an elderly person has fallen in the shower—or on her kitchen floor—and ends up lying there for hours before someone just happens to discover her. Younger people laugh at these cheesy commercials. The line has been the punch line of countless comedy sketches and stand-up routines. But people who find themselves suddenly past 65, or adult children of parents in their 80s, don't laugh anymore—even though they may have thought these ads were ridiculous a few decades ago. It's suddenly not funny; it's terrifying.

What makes Life Alert's marketing so successful is that it taps directly into a primal emotion of its intended customer:

fear. When you are a senior, the fear of falling and being alone, in pain, for hours or days is as terrifying as *Jaws* was to people afraid to swim in the ocean. The odds of falling when you're over 65 are dramatically greater than being eaten by a shark at any age. According to the Center for Disease Control (CDC), one third of people over 65 will fall every year. In 2008, according to the CDC's website, almost 20,000 seniors died from falls. But it's not the statistics that make the Life Alert campaign so successful, it's the vivid thought of you lying there in horrible pain, all alone, unable to get to a phone for help. It's pure fear—one of the primary emotions.

The Life Alert marketing campaign is a perfect example of emotions playing a primary role in persuasion. We may, as the homo sapient species, pride ourselves that we act rationally; that we are unmoved by marketing messages and make decisions based on facts alone. But we're deluding ourselves. We are as run by our emotions as the most screaming, vegetation-tearing troop of chimpanzees Jane Goodall ever observed.

ALL MARKETS ARE EMOTIONAL

The truth is that all of us humans, regardless of our credentials, intelligence, profession, education, or gender (yes, men, you too) are emotional creatures. Our emotions are the boss of us. Even thoughtful, educated people, stating the need for data and technical specifications, are driven by a deeper need to be reassured that they're not making a colossal mistake. Emotions are right under the surface of every rational decision. Understand this fact and you can persuade anyone.

The second thing to understand about marketing with emotion is that when you can put someone into an emotional state, they are more open to suggestion. That sounds very crass and manipulative, and it can be used both for good and evil, but when we are aroused by emotion, our senses are heightened, our attention is acute, and our neural activity is running at a fever pitch. We're all ears.

You can see this working all around you. In a political campaign where a candidate is charismatic, emotions are the target. He uses selective "facts" to drive enthusiasm. His charisma, in fact, is nothing more than the ability of that candidate to tap into an emotional state. Look at the 2004 U.S. presidential election, when the incumbent, George W. Bush, was running against a tidal wave of electoral frustration, you would have thought he was a dead man walking. Yet with two endless wars, a staggering deficit, a stagnant economy, and unprecedented unpopularity, Bush still beat his opponent, John Kerry, who had all the "facts" on his side. The difference was emotion. During debates and in speeches, Kerry's speaking style was all data. He never gave a straight, simple answer but spoke in a monotonic, reasonable tone, looking at every side of a question until people's eyes glazed over. He was Spock. By contrast, Bush used his studied, aw-shucks folksiness to get ordinary people to identify with him, in spite of how mad so many of them were with his administration. They felt he was one of them. He never talked down to them, never pretended to be one of those Ivy League snobs (even though both he and Kerry went to Yale together), and even attempted to show that he had a sense of humor. He was more emotionally approachable. He was Captain Kirk. As a result, even though the race was close, the candidate with all the "facts" on his side lost to the one with emotional appeal.

EMOTION IS THE BOSS OF REASON

In the chapter on Rule #3, Be Creative or Die, we talked about how evoking an emotion can make it easier to get through to a customer. But it is also vital in establishing an emotional bond. For example, if you make someone laugh (on purpose), they'll tend to like you. You've just given them a gift; a joke. It's disarming. You not only have their attention, you now have their affinity, possibly their loyalty, too. When they are predisposed to like you, they're more likely to want to do business with you. And that, in a nutshell, is how to start building brand loyalty.

Even brands that you'd never suspect of having an emotional connection with their customers have one nonetheless. If you're a scientific instruments company, for example, and your customers are scientists and engineers, you've got a tough crowd. Here are highly educated people who pride themselves on their immunity from squishy things like emotion. Everything they do is based on hard, reproducible experiment. One of the most common signs in an engineer's cubicle is W. E. Deming's famous quote, "In God we trust. All others bring data." For that reason they also smugly proclaim their immunity from the blandishments of marketing. Just give them the facts and they'll make their decision based on that. And yet we have watched scores of engineers and PhDs in focus groups get very emotional about their attachment to certain brands of mass spectrometers and function generators. Of course, they always have ready-to-go, good, technical reasons why they are so biased. But these data are only served up to justify their emotional preference.

A client of ours, who also happens to be an engineer, is very frank about this denial of emotion among his colleagues. He has a phrase for manipulating the emotional preferences of a technical customer. He calls it "The Illusion of Data." Point to the "specs"—processing speed, throughput capacity, signal-to-noise ratio, it doesn't matter—put them in the form of a graph or a chart, and you're done. It doesn't matter what the specs are, because bigger, faster, smaller, all mean better. He recognized that most engineers and scientists will have already made an emotional decision about a brand of instrument anyway. They feel more comfortable with certain brands. They just need to be able to point to a number to justify the ineffable, emotional reason for that preference. They might prefer Agilent mass spectrometers, for instance, because they can talk about the accuracy of the output, but the real reason is something they would never admit; they just feel more comfortable working with Agilent; they've always worked with Agilent (from as long ago as when it was Hewlett-Packard); the logo on the instrument's faceplate reassures them as much as their "Mr. Blankey did" when they were toddlers. Agilent never lets them down.

This Illusion-of-Data technique even works on non-technical customers buying high-tech products. Amateur photographers shopping for a digital camera are conditioned to look for megapixels (more means better), even though that spec alone has less to do with the quality of the picture than other things like the lens or the sensor. Buyers of laptops want to know how much RAM, how much storage, how fast the clock speed of the processor is. But they just need a number to justify the emotional need to plop down $1,200 for a shiny new toy, with Intel inside, or that glowing Apple logo on the lid.

It doesn't matter what the product or service is; people will make a decision about it emotionally in a fraction of the time it takes them to work out the supporting reasons. Then they'll cherry pick the data that support their emotional decision. Be honest: have you ever looked at the Consumer Reports specs for a computer or flat screen TV and then felt yourself disappointed that the best rated one wasn't the brand that you had your heart set on? Or that it was a brand you never heard of? Or, on the other hand, have you ever decided on a new model of car, and felt the elation of validation when you find out it has the best safety rating, or the highest MPG numbers in its class? In truth, the smell, feel, and look of the car in a showroom has more to do with sales than MPG or J. D. Power ratings.

WHAT EMOTIONS SHOULD WE USE?

The most effective emotions for marketing are the eight most primitive: humor, fear, trust, guilt, affection, hunger, sex, envy. Psychologists, depending on their particular theoretical bias, may argue about whether hunger or trust are really emotions. But we're talking about marketing, not academics. By emotions we mean: Do you feel something? And when you're hungry, you definitely feel it. When you trust or distrust somebody, there's definitely a feeling in the pit of your stomach.

So, what follows are the most effective feelings, emotions, or "amygdalagenic altered states" you can use. Whatever you want to call them, Dr. Muckenfuss.

HUMOR

The easiest and most common emotion is humor. Humor is so pervasive in human culture that it is sometimes not recognized as an emotional state itself. But the particular feeling evoked by a funny or silly situation is distinct from generic joy. The laughter caused by humor evokes a definite feeling that transcends mere well-being. It is more like being tickled from inside.

Humor is extremely powerful. Make somebody laugh and you've got them right where you want them. Odysseus, the eponymous hero of *The Odyssey*, knew this instinctively 2,800 years ago when he made the Cyclops, Polyphemus, laugh so he wouldn't eat him (at least until last; Polyphemus ate the less funny shipmates first). Humor is an ancient sales ploy. But it's also useful in circumstances other than trying not to get eaten. When you make someone laugh, you disarm them; you give them a little gift. It feels good to laugh, and we are more likely to want to listen to someone who cracks us up. It's why speakers so typically start with a joke; so the audience won't eat them.

The vast majority of memorable commercials are humorous ones. The most forgettable commercials are just informative. There is undoubtedly a neurobiological reason for this, but it's also something that we all know from personal experience. More people can recite lines from Monty Python movies than statistics from documentaries about global warming.

Under Rule #6, Give Love to Get Love, using humor also shows respect for your audience. Since nobody likes to be interrupted or sold to, telling a little joke is like a peace offering; something to atone for the interruption. When a company makes you laugh, you tend to like them. It reveals a more human, generous side to them. You tend to think, these guys would be fun to do business with. They're not so deadly serious. You're also more likely to forgive them for interrupting you. And you pay attention.

Comedy is where viral marketing was born. People are more inclined, in this age of social networking, to send funny ads to friends. How many dull commercials are forwarded versus funny ones? Humor can enlist your customers as your own sales force, not to mention turbo-charging your media reach.

Humor is one of the most powerful forces in the universe (since it's a flavor of love). That was proven scientifically in the Pixar movie, *Monsters, Inc.* It should be used responsibly and wisely, grasshopper.

FEAR

Another tried and tested emotion used in marketing is fear. Not terror, per se; there are not many ad campaigns that scare the willies out of people (aside from trailers for horror movies). But there are tons of ads that make people worry about acne, depression, retirement, home invasion, identity theft, dandruff, smoking, data loss, erectile dysfunction, damaged hair, falling down, or anything to throw a bucket of ice in the warm bliss that governs the average person's life. There's a lot to be scared of.

Fear is not as effective in disarming a viewer as humor. Not only are you interrupted; you're interrupted rudely, with a frightening thought that your zit is going to turn your face into an alien monster. So, as far as stopping someone from scanning through the commercial, fear isn't that effective. But it has its uses.

As an emotion, fear is very effective in getting someone to listen to your message. Fear makes us start pumping adrenalin. Our lives may depend on it. At least our social lives. The Life Alert "I've Fallen and I Can't Get Up!" campaign is a perfect example of using fear to get a message remembered. But an acne cream commercial testifying to the teenage horrors of social rejection is equally effective.

A classic example of fear from the annals of political advertising is Doyle Dane Bernbach's 1964 TV commercial for presidential candidate Lyndon Johnson, featuring an adorable little girl picking the petals off of a flower while she counts. When she picks the last petal and looks up, an atomic bomb goes off. An announcer says, "Vote for

President Johnson on November 3rd. The stakes are too high for you to stay home."

The ad ran for only one day. The Republican Party protested the unfairness and tastelessness of the ad, so the Democrats took it off. But it only needed to run once. The point was made. The Republican challenger, Barry Goldwater, had been running on a "get tough with Communism" platform and had been painted as a dangerous extremist by the Democrats. Goldwater's own campaign slogan, "Extremism in the Defense of Liberty Is No Vice," as well as his statements that atomic weapons should not be categorically ruled out in Vietnam, didn't exactly help his brand image, either.

After the brief airing of the ad, and its controversial pulling, the endless commentary about it on the news channels made it "viral" before "viral" was even a marketing term (another example of Rule #4, The Message is the Medium). The inflammatory ad, appearing just weeks before the election, was enough to cause doubt in so many people that Johnson won in the most lopsided landslide ever. To this day, the "Daisy" ad, as it was called, is rated as one of the most memorable advertising messages in history, undoubtedly changing history itself.

Of course fear is the most common emotion exploited in political advertising. It is far easier, in such a polemical choice, to make the electorate fear your opponent than love you, because the choice is made only once. It takes a long time to build a bond of love, but only one, vivid idea to generate fear. The belief that a candidate is trustworthy and has everyone's best interest at heart is not nearly so motivating as the fear that his opponent might end the world as we know it.

But fear, in less terrifying levels than nuclear holocaust, has also been used with great effect in the commercial realm. There is a legend in advertising that a marketing war between white tuna canners and pink tuna canners began with the white meat canners claiming that their product "Doesn't turn pink in the can." Whether the ad campaign actually ran or not (and many old ad pundits claim they swear seeing it during their lifetimes), the tale is a very good illustration of the use of unfounded fear of the competition to promote a product. Of course, no tuna turns pink in the can; it's either pink or white going in. But the claim that the white tuna won't turn pink in the can puts an unfair onus on the pink packers. "What's wrong with pink tuna?" consumers would ask themselves. "What's wrong with the cans?" "Is white tuna a sign of freshness?" And so on. The apocryphal "white tuna" marketers generated an artificial and irrational fear—that pinkness is a sign of contamination—to cause people to prefer their tuna over the competitor's.

TRUST

Trust is also a pliable emotion. When you trust someone, you feel comfortable falling backwards into their arms—no looking! You're comfortable. You feel safe. Trust can be thought of as the opposite emotion to fear.

In marketing, whether you're marketing a product or marketing yourself, building up that emotional trust can be a very powerful persuader. It is particularly useful in creating a brand preference for an established commodity, like cars, insurance, soap, or soup.

Volvo has carefully nurtured the emotion of trust in its audience for decades. The brand has come to stand for engineering—engineering for safety. Early Volvo ads even used the perceived ugliness of its car design to represent that trust. Yeah, it's boxy. But it's safe.

Likewise, Allstate Insurance, has built its brand around the trust motive; "You're in Good Hands." The narrative of its marketing has always been based on demonstrations of Allstate being there when it matters.

And Campbell's Soup has long established a trust metaphor between its brand and your mother, the ultimate in trust-worthy symbols. Eating Campbell's Soup is the equivalent of having your own mother feed you…assuming your mother fed you.

All three companies, Volvo, Allstate, and Campbell's Soup, might be considered commodities in their respective markets. But they've all used the comforting emotion that comes with trust to make themselves strong brands.

Trust can also work to sustain a brand even after there's a perfectly good—and cheaper—generic version. The patent on aspirin (acetylsalicylic acid, a synthetic version of an ancient pain reliever from willow bark) expired almost a hundred years ago. But Bayer, the company that first developed Aspirin (the original brand name of the drug), has ever since used that original claim to reinforce the trust of its loyal customers, allowing it to still retain a 14.6% share of the aspirin market almost a century after its patent expired.

Generic, brandless aspirin can be had at a rock-bottom price, but the brand name Bayer has come to stand for the "real thing" over generations, even though the chemical formula is essentially the same.

Another example of leveraging the emotion of trust is the "Intel Inside" campaign. Intel does not make computers. It makes the components of computers. When you buy a computer you're buying a Mac, HP, Toshiba, Sony, or IBM; not an Intel. But by partnering with key computer manufacturers to co-brand their products with the secret ingredient of Intel processors inside, Intel actually created a preference for those models which had the little Intel Inside sticker on the keyboard. Why would anyone care? When you buy a computer, or a car, or any highly sophisticated appliance, you shouldn't care where the parts come from, right? Intel made sure that you would care.

Intel, the original inventor of the x86 microprocessor, was to semiconductors what Bayer was to pain relievers. So it was a stroke of marketing genius to recognize that creating a demand for the branded guts of a computer would help all boats to rise. The implication is, if the brain of a computer is made by Intel, you can trust it. So you feel safe buying it. They don't call it a motherboard for nothing.

GUILT

Speaking of mothers, this is the emotion they know how to push the best. We are all guilty of using guilt to get people to do things for us, or of allowing ourselves to be compelled to do things. As a persuasion tool guilt is the most effective emotion in most families. You lend money to your brother, not because you trust him, not because he makes you laugh, not because you're afraid of him (though you may be), but because he's your brother, and that's what families do. It's guilt.

Guilt is also useful in commercial marketing. Charities are adept at poking our guilt by showing images of starving children, abused animals, and suffering young mothers. It is the most appropriate emotion for raising donations.

It is also useful for less obvious persuasion. Aside from trust, Volvo's implied, secondary emotional stick is guilt. Just look at the line of cars waiting to pick up kids at an upscale elementary school and count the Volvos. Driving your family around in anything but a Volvo borders on the criminally negligent. Do you want to maim your children in a car accident? What kind of a parent are you?

McDonald's, in altering their Happy Meals to give parents the option of fresh fruit instead of fries, assuaged the guilt of those parents who felt they could give into their kids' incessant nagging for McDonald's without feeling like they were harming their health. It's a win-win! At least emotionally. If they ignore the deep fried McNuggets and caramel. And maybe the kids won't nag so much if they know they're going to have to eat apples. This is also an example of McDonald's obeying Rule #6, loving their customers.

Guilt is good.

AFFECTION
Affection can include feelings of nurturing, what we feel

when we see puppies and babies, or when we're made to think of our family or spouse. Many marketers shamelessly stroke this emotion to get you to buy life insurance, or adopt an abused animal, or put on your seat belt.

The already-mentioned "Embrace Life" video from Sussex, England, with the father being saved by the arms of his daughter and wife, is a good example of using affection to change behavior. If you have a family, the commercial, besides exploiting the fear of loss, reminds you of your warm feelings for them. It reminds you how much other people need you.

But we're also all familiar, too, with commercials like the Humane Society's in which Sarah McLaughlin begs us to help abused animals. We hear her sing a plaintive song (in a minor key, of course) over heart-rending photos of helpless and maimed animals looking imploringly at us. No one with a heart can see that commercial and not feel pity…at least no one any of us would have anything to do with.

Affection can also be layered subtly on top of humor. The famous E*Trade ad campaign with the snarky-talking baby, besides making us laugh and remember that trading with E*Trade is so easy that even an infant could do it, also reminds us that we need to think about planning for the future because…well…that little guy is just so damn cute!

HUNGER

Hunger is the most primitive of all emotions. All carbon-based life forms share it, from bacteria to Bruce Springsteen. It's an ancient and insidious marketing lever.

It is also the one of the most powerful emotions to market with—if you're marketing food, that is.

Food companies, both packaged foods and restaurants, use the hunger emotion to not only create a brand preference, but to create a need in the first place. This is why they spare no expense (if they're smart) in photographing food the way it only appears in heaven. Squads of food stylists are hired to fuss over the dishes to look just so, using professional tricks to get our gastric juices squirting. Photographers spend hours finessing the light to bring out the best colors, to hit that steak with highlights, to bring out the glistening drops of dew on the apple. All this work is painstakingly done because food advertisers know that the way to the stomach is through the eyes. You see an image like that and your stomach starts growling. You have to eat. Now.

We once developed an outdoor billboard campaign for McDonald's in Southern California to promote key menu items (Big Mac,® Quarter Pounder,® and McD.L.T.®). As an experiment, we proposed that we run the billboards without any copy, just the big, juicy product images and the McDonald's logo. No expense was spared to make the burgers look as inviting as possible. And the copywriter showed admirable restraint in refraining from writing clever, pun-filled headlines. But the results of the campaign were dramatic. Measured traffic into McDonald's stores went up markedly during the run of the campaign, even though no words told people to go to McDonald's. As if hypnotized, and with nothing between their eyes and those seductive images of juicy burgers, people thronged into McDonalds to obey their primitive emotion.

Beyond advertising, though, leveraging hunger is used in all aspects of food marketing. Menus of chain restaurants are lavished with professional food photography, as are menu boards at fast food stores. Food packaging is also carefully designed with hunger-inducing images. The exhaust vents of burger restaurants, pizza parlors, and bakeries serve as hunger cues by pumping the smell of charbroiled meat and baked bread into the neighborhood. Food marketers even use certain colors, scientifically calibrated to spark a hunger response. Reds and yellows predominate in burger chains (suggesting red meat), greens in gourmet grocery stores (suggesting fresh produce). All of the senses are stimulated, anything to get people to come in and order the Super Size Meal.

SEX

Watch it! There are children present.

Sex—or more precisely, sexual arousal—is the second most primitive emotion and perhaps the most well known in marketing. Sexual stimulation is often derided as being immoral and exploitive. There is so much of morality and religious taboo associated with sex that it is uncomfortable to even acknowledge it in our culture. And yet sex is, all the same, pervasive. It is something no responsible marketer should ignore, even though red-faced.

The most obvious examples of sex in marketing are in fashion and fragrance advertising. While some seem just this side of pornographic in suggestiveness, most of the images show extremely young, extremely attractive, extremely sensuous people in their prime of health and vigor. The emotional lever is similar to that of hunger; these images are designed to arouse. You're supposed to be thinking of sex when you see the big displays of half-naked men and women in Abercrombie & Fitch or Victoria's Secret. But at the same time, you're supposed to be thinking, "That could be me; I could be that attractive. If only I wore these frayed jeans. They're $179, but I'm worth it!"

The utility of sex in fashion advertising is so evident that it needs no elaboration. But sex is used in all sorts of marketing that has nothing to do with reproduction. It's about making yourself look good, which is ultimately all about marketing yourself personally. When restaurant commercials are shot, or insurance commercials, or even air freshener ads, have you noticed how they always use young, attractive people? That's because young, attractive people are more persuasive than old, average-looking people. Producers spend days casting for the best looking young girl to take a bite out of that barbecued chicken sandwich. Biologically, they know that someone who looks sexually attractive (even with all of their clothes on) is going to be more persuasive. Don't fight it. That's the way we are.

Even in a recent Carl's Jr. commercial, the spot self-referentially and unapologetically acknowledges that they use hot, sexy models in their ads because, as they say, "Ugly ones don't sell burgers." The humor in this is that it touches on an embarrassing truth about us.

Of course this kind of marketing is also something we

indulge in on a personal level. The very reason women spend billions on cosmetics is so they can market themselves, not just to men but to each other. It's a competitive thing. It's also a self-esteem thing, as we try to convince ourselves, we are still attractive, damn it! If it weren't for personal marketing, there would be no cosmetics industry, no fashion industry, no personal fitness industry. Let's face it, we crunch abs not to be more fit, but to get laid—or at least not to be embarrassed in a bathing suit.

ENVY

Closely related to sex is the emotion of envy.

Another reason marketers prefer to cast young, healthy, sexy people in their ads is that people envy youth and health. They want to be those people. The ads say to us, if you drive this car, if you drink this coffee, if you trade with this brokerage firm, if you use this shampoo, you can be young and healthy again, just like these people—as irrational as we know that is.

Even in marketing that is specifically about sex, the images of health, attractiveness and vigor are vital. The average user of Viagra or Cialis does not look like the silver-haired Adonis in the advertising. His wife (we assume it's supposed to be his wife) probably does not look like that wholesome-but-still-hot actress. But in the mind of the guy who is about to pick up the phone and call that 1-800 number, Viagra will make him look that good. And healthy.

Wealth is another image that elicits envy for the same reason. It is something to aspire to because it brings power, good looks, health, sexual prowess, and respect. And, if you're wealthy, you'll never have to work another day in your life.

So, the emotional line goes: if you use our brand, you'll be all that you desire. It's like your personal genie in a bottle.

If you let reason step in, though, you'll work out that the argument is ridiculous. Driving a Mercedes is not going to make you rich (quite the opposite if you really can't afford one), but it will communicate your personal marketing message that you are wealthy enough, and discerning enough, to drive one. The brand of the car says so much about you to the rest of the world.

When the iPad came out, its biggest emotional draw was envy. The first people who had iPads were envied by their peers. People would stand in line outside the Apple store for hours to buy one, hoping the store wouldn't run out. It was just another appliance, a big iPhone (without the phone part). But envy of those who had one when you didn't was what drove the market.

Even something as dry as a brokerage company can provoke envy in its audience. The most common scenario in a financial services commercial is to show people retiring in some exotic location, snuggling with their spouse (the same wholesome-but-still-hottie of the Viagra commercials) in front of a fire or on a beach, or tinkering with a vintage car. Every image is designed to elicit an envious response; "I want to be that guy!" How? "Let these guys give me financial advice. What's that website again?"

Of course, these spots are not directed at the young

gluttons stuffing their faces at a Carl's Jr. They're directed at people who are getting close to retirement and, in all likelihood, already too late to be planning for it. So the envy is working on steroids. The magic promise is, if you haven't done anything about your retirement yet, we can help you live like this cool rich guy tinkering with his vintage Mustang at his house in Malibu—alongside his trophy wife, of course.

Envy is an emotion that can work wonders.

DON'T ABANDON REASON

This is not to say you should abandon reason in obeying Rule #7. Reason is very useful for shoring up the emotional decision. As we pointed out before, the self-image of most rational people is that they make decisions based on the facts. Even though they may make up their minds early on about buying a car, they need those hard specs (the J. D. Power ratings) to justify the decision. Few people are going to admit to themselves, when they buy a new car, "I don't know; it just made me feel sexy." They also need to have the mileage data at their fingertips.

Cold hard facts can also build a case for an emotional response. Volvo could not have earned credibility as the safest car on the road had they not put in the hard engineering and had the statistics to back up that claim. They just didn't arbitrarily start labeling themselves as the world's safest automobile. They had to put their entire shoulder behind it. They had to live it. In other words, they had to consciously make the world's safest automobile as the foundation of their entire brand. So the emotionally evocative claim to safety is reinforced by reason—and facts.

Even in something as subjective as cosmetic marketing, there are objective reasons backing the emotional response of looking more attractive. Cosmetics have been developed by chemists and professionals over centuries to create the optimum effect on the body. There is science behind cosmetics. And knowing that there is science involved, women become technical experts about the cosmetics they buy. And with that knowledge, they feel more trust in using them. This, in turn, makes them more self-confident (an emotion itself), which also makes them more attractive.

It is the same with someone who buys a particular brand of car. Knowing certain details of the engineering and design enhances the emotional feel of driving it. Or to someone retouching a photo on their Mac, knowing technical details about why they bought the Mac, makes them feel more self-assured using it. It is reason at the service of emotion. And, at the same time, it is the emotion that makes the reason meaningful.

LIVING WITH YOURSELF

It's okay to be manipulative. It's even okay to manipulate emotions. All manipulation is a way to persuade someone to listen to you, and even to buy what you're trying to sell them, whether it's an idea or a brand of toothpaste. Many people think it is somehow dishonest or evil to push emotional buttons in the service of commerce, but it's in our very chromosomes to be emotional communicators.

Any persuasive technique can be used for ill. It's not the

technique, however, that makes it wrong, it's the intent. We're not suggesting you be dishonest. We're just saying that if you are aware of the tremendous power of emotion in marketing, you'll be more persuasive.

You may ask someone to marry you using a long, rational argument. But if she isn't sold on the idea emotionally before you start your PowerPoint presentation, your argument will sail off into space, Mr. Spock.

You may have an equally long, well-thought-out argument for why you'd be perfect for a job. But if the person in a position to hire you has a bad feeling about you in the first place, you won't get it.

And you may have charts and graphs demonstrating why your burger is more tasty and nutritious than any other, but if you don't make your customer salivate at the very sight of it, he won't buy it.

It's okay to have rational arguments, as long as they are underpinned by a strong, emotional appeal.

It's also okay to buy something just because you like it. Liking it is the whole point.

>DO THIS

Use emotions to motivate. Facts and figures will never move people the way emotions can. When people are moved, they move.

UNBREAKABLE RULE #8

GO BIG OR
GO HOME

WANNA GO TO THE MOON, ALICE?

"This nation should commit itself to achieving the goal, before the decade is out, of landing a man on the moon and returning him safely to the earth."—President John F. Kennedy addressing Congress, May 25th, 1961.

When Kennedy set that goal, one of the biggest leaps of imagination in the history of our planet, we hadn't even successfully got a human being into space yet. In fact, it had been only 58 years since the first successful flight of a powered aircraft at Kitty Hawk. And now we were already promising to go to the moon? What were we? Nuts?

This is what we mean by going big. It may have been crazy, but as we all know now, we did it. In fact, it may have been our craziness itself that made it possible.

Go back a little further, say a few hundred thousand years. We find some very smart, very tough, but very literal-minded creatures called Neanderthals who were surviving by their wits and grit through a long ice age. They were some of the smartest creatures the planet had ever seen. We know from fossils of their skulls that their brains were probably bigger than ours. And they could've undoubtedly beaten the tar out of us in a bar fight. But they had no imagination. For almost a quarter of a million years they made essentially the same sort of stone tools without improvement. Their technology was elegant, but no more elegant than a bird's nest or a termite mound or a beaver dam. They had no art. There is debate about whether they could even talk. They were the epitome of conservatives. But they had survived for over 200,000 years in some pretty harsh conditions. So they must have been doing something right. At least they were following Rule #1, Consistency Beats Ability.

But very shortly after another very smart primate started showing up in Europe and Asia, the Neanderthals started dying out. These new, skinny creatures were probably thought of as crazy by the Neanderthals. They painted pictures on the walls of caves. They kept inventing new devices to help them compete and tame the world. They hunted mammoths and woolly rhinos, for crying out loud! They even ventured out across the ocean in little wooden boats. No Neanderthal in his right mind would ever attempt these foolhardy things. It just wasn't done.

But our ancestors showed them. Within only a thousand generations of the first modern humans walking out of Africa, we were walking on the moon. Take that, Neanderthals!

Oh wait. They can't. They're extinct.

Which is just the point. Not to put a chauvinistic message on it, but the lesson here is that we imaginative bipeds—the ones who thought big enough to cross the ocean in flimsy, wooden boats, go after really big game, and boldly go where no primate had gone before—we thought big and went big. We occupied every part of the planet, and then some. We made pyramids and symphonies and plays and airplanes and spandex and scanning electronic microscopes and large hadron colliders and the Internet. We ruled.

Of course the Neanderthals are still among us, in spirit if not genetically. And undoubtedly there were some whiners among the early bands of migrating modern humans—the ones who wanted to know "what was wrong with staying right here?" They were the guys who only saw problems. They regarded themselves as the voice of reason. You probably even work with some of them to this day. They're the ones who would not only say, "Don't rock the boat!" but "Don't get in the boat in the first place!"

Why is this object lesson about the Neanderthals a rule of marketing? Because the same rule that applies to natural selection of species applies to the natural selection of companies. The companies that get big are the ones who go big. And stay big. And all of them, like the tiny handful of homo sapiens who walked north from Africa a thousand generations ago, started off as small companies; sometimes in somebody's garage. Or cave.

The rule is: If you're going to grow your business, or further your cause, or just improve your life, you have to think past where you are now. And you have to go all out with everything that you do. This especially includes your marketing.

RAISE YOUR SIGHTS

The first place to start thinking big is in the potential for your own business. Many enterprises are content to keep reaching out to the same customers they always have. When you ask them about who their market is, they invariably come back with who is currently buying their product. That's fine. But that's thinking small. And, harsh as it may be to say, those customers are eventually going to die. It's just a fact of life.

What you really need to do is think about who isn't buying your product yet. You need to imagine how much of the world doesn't even know about you. Set your sights on all of those people. Your loyal customer base will take care of itself. It's okay if you have lofty, even ridiculous goals and come up short. Even if you only get halfway there, you're much further than if you hadn't even tried. Don't limit your growth to the height of your ceiling; raise the ceiling.

If Kennedy's challenge in 1961 had merely been, "This nation should commit itself to achieving the goal, before the decade is out, of flying a man nonstop to California and returning him safely to Washington," would we have ever made it to the moon? Or would we have enjoyed the huge economic boom that was a result of the Space Race?

A well-known marketing tale of what can happen when a company decides to raise its sights is Arm & Hammer. Up until the 1970s, the company made garden-variety baking soda; just ordinary sodium bicarbonate ($NaHCO3$), soda ash, used mostly in...well...baking. Since the time of the Pharaohs this simple compound had been primarily used to make bread rise and soothe indigestion. Of course, people knew of all sorts of other homey uses for baking soda from their moms and dads. But it wasn't until the 1970s that Arm & Hammer started to capitalize on the widespread utility of this simple chemical and literally think outside of the orange box.

The company began collecting all of the homespun applications of its soda and started branding and marketing them. We saw Arm & Hammer laundry soap, toothpaste, underarm deodorant, kitty litter, room deodorizers, rug cleaners, fabric softeners, air filters, and stain removers. We were exposed to useful advertising tips about sticking a box of Arm & Hammer in our refrigerators to suck up the odor of that Chinese takeout we should have gotten rid of weeks before. We learned about pouring Arm & Hammer over the crusty terminals of our car batteries to neutralize the acid buildup. We found out we should keep a box on hand to put out pesky kitchen fires. We learned that we could use it in diaper pails to keep from gagging whenever we changed our babies.

The Arm & Hammer website talks about pouring it in our pools or spas to regulate pH and kill algae. It also advises us to pour it down the drain every week to keep our septic systems healthy. We can use it to clean our barbecue grills and our cars' grills. In fact, there are so many uses for this simple stuff that it seems like there is almost nothing Arm & Hammer baking soda can't do. We wonder what it would do for our love life (aside from the obvious benefits of toothpaste and deodorant).

Arm & Hammer is the model for raising your marketing sights. It is the simplest of products with countless uses. And it's managed to brand itself, with its 165-year-old orange and red box, as the indispensable but simple product with a thousand virtues. The marketing wizards at Arm & Hammer looked at their otherwise dry product and thought, "Who else can we sell to?" Also, "What else can we do with this stuff?"

But it's just baking soda. Did you know you could even bake with it?

PULL THE TRIGGER

A big idea alone isn't good enough. Every year thousands of great marketing ideas are shelved out of timidity. For every marketing campaign that finally runs, there are a dozen that were conceived but never produced. But what's worse is all those campaigns that were produced but had so little exposure that they died from lack of light, like a plant you put in the closet and forget to water. And to return to our original space-race metaphor, we didn't just build the spaceships and leave them on the launch pad; we went to the moon with them.

Great marketing messages aren't magic spells. You can't come up with the perfect creative tagline, whisper it in a dark, secret ceremony, and expect the customers to start flocking to your website. You have to shout it from the rooftops— or at least on YouTube. You have to advertise. You have to get the word out. And sometimes you have to put your money where your mouth is. There's no free shortcut; viral marketing notwithstanding. Viral marketing can certainly multiply your media reach if your message is strong enough (or funny enough), but if no one knows about it in the first place, it ain't goin' nowhere. Zero times anything is still zero.

Years ago we helped a large packaged foods company (which shall remain nameless because, well, you'll see...) develop a campaign to introduce a brand new line of par-baked, gourmet pizzas to the North American market. The pizzas were quite good and did very well in market testing. The pizza factory was up and running. The distribution system was all worked out. The grocery store relationships were spiffed. And we actually produced three, thirty-second TV spots to advertise these pizzas nationally. Everything was ready to go.

Then they decided to do some focus groups.

We showed the spots to the groups and they were generally liked. But the person in charge of Product Branding was worried. There was something...hmm, something he just couldn't put his finger on. He didn't know why, but the ads weren't perfect yet. So he put the whole thing on hold until he figured out what was missing.

The spots never aired. The pizzas were never introduced to the market. And other less timid competitors like California Pizza Kitchen and Wolfgang Puck eventually introduced their own par-baked, gourmet pizzas, "beating" our client to into supermarkets years later. You may not be surprised to hear that this same packaged foods company was the very one described under Rule # 3, Be Creative or Die; the one that needed to have its cat food commercials show the cat licking its chops exactly twice. This company was almost religiously committed to its magic marketing formulae, so much so that, even armed with strong market research, they couldn't find the guts to take a leap and go big with a new product.

The biggest mistake that our timid pizza maker made was in thinking small. They looked upon the risks of introducing a new product as if it were just another line of spaghetti sauce or boxed macaroni. They failed to see that they had the potential to create an entirely new product category, and to seize the high ground before anyone else caught on. Instead, they left the high ground to smaller companies like Wolfgang Puck and California Pizza Kitchen, and missed a huge opportunity.

The lesson here is that you have to think big and jump. Of course there are risks. There are always risks. But there are risks from inaction, too, as our would-be pizza maker found out. And there are always going to be people (with traces of that Neanderthal genome) who see only the downside. It's wise to listen to those people, but sometimes you need to recognize that their advice may come more from fear of the unknown than prudence. When someone in your entourage says, "But what if somebody doesn't like it?" slap them. Metaphorically, of course.

THINKING REALLY BIG

And there are true visionaries who thought big by going far beyond what had always been done before; those who saw innovations in technology and how they could transform civilization itself. When early telephones were introduced in the late 1870s, the new technology was originally conceived as useful only for businesses. But Bell Telephone had a big-thinking marketing genius in its first general manager, Theodore Vail, who realized by 1900 that the device, originally developed for business, could also be used in the home. "No it couldn't," said the Neanderthals of the day, the conventional thinkers. "Who would want to talk to someone over a phone if they weren't doing business?" Besides, it would require an enormous investment in infrastructure—wires, operator exchanges, switching technology, power supplies. But Vail said, "So?" and pushed to make telephones available to anyone who wanted one. The investment was made. The rest is history. The world was changed as a result. People could suddenly speak directly to someone three thousand miles away as if they were in the same room. That was thinking big.

Exactly one hundred years later, the same big thinking was applied to another for-business-only device, the personal computer. In 1977 the dynamic Steves, Wozniak and Jobs, designed and marketed one of the first personal computers for home use, the Apple II. Six years later Apple did it again by introducing the first mass-produced personal computer with a graphical WYSIWYG (for What You See Is What You Get) interface, the Macintosh. "The computer for the rest of us," was its brand message. Of course companies, including Xerox, HP, and IBM, had been ahead of Apple in microcomputer design, and even WYSIWIG interface technology, but the difference was Jobs' idea of the end user. By going beyond the conventional business machine user and thinking of "the rest of us," he had created a whole new market and an entirely new era in civilization. This was thinking big with a vengeance. And today Apple is ranked as one of the most valuable companies on the planet.

Only a decade after this big idea that computers could be personal, another visionary, Senator Al Gore, had the big idea that if the government opened up its fledgling digital information network (previously called ARPANET, for Advanced Research Projects Agency Network) for everyone's use, it could be a good thing. Up until the late 1980s, primitive computer networks had been accessed only by certain academic institutions and government agencies. But Gore thought, if everyone could use this infrastructure— what he liked to call the "information superhighway"—then it would benefit the whole world, not just a few academics and bureaucrats in their ivory towers. By pushing through the passage of the High Performance Computing and Communications Act of 1991, Gore launched a digital information revolution, whose child was the Internet, the biggest idea to affect civilization since the invention of the printing press over five hundred years earlier.

But we're not done yet. Within ten years, three other visionaries, Sergey Brin, Larry Page and Jimmy Wales, all saw that the Internet could be used to revolutionize the way information was organized and accessed. For centuries human knowledge was amassed in institutions like libraries; physical vaults of books and documents, organized by catalogues. Encyclopedias were a single set of volumes condensing all of the established knowledge of mankind, edited by respected experts in their particular fields. Anyone old enough to remember the Dewey Decimal System also remembers going to the library to look things up for a school paper, or tediously cribbing a report due the next day from the family encyclopedia.

Now the Internet comes along, but by itself it doesn't do much to change the way information was hunted. It had been described as the world's largest library, with all the books thrown in a big heap on the floor. But Brin, Page, and Wales each had a hand in changing all that.

With the invention of the Google search engine, Brin and Page created a concept that made old libraries obsolete. Instead of spending hours poring over books at the local library, an average person could now take only seconds to find what they were looking for in what amounted to, the universal library of all human civilization. Writing term papers, finding obscure objects, looking up odd facts, verifying outrageous claims, settling bets, locating out-of-print books, researching investments, and filling countless other weird cravings for knowledge, could, thanks to Google, happen in a snap.

Then, with Wikipedia, Jimmy Wales invented a peer-reviewed hyper-encyclopedia, rendering all previous concepts of encyclopedias as quaint as the Dead Sea Scrolls. Early objections to Wikipedia by old world scholars were that the information contained within was unverifiable and not edited by the best authorities in their fields. But the evolving editorial discipline of Wikipedia insured that only recognized authorities in their respective fields could make changes. The information became peer-reviewed.

The additional advantage of Wikipedia, too, was that it allowed for controversial arguments to be aired, not just the academically dominant view. So people could look at all aspects of an idea. Unlike the *Encyclopedia Britannica*, you could find up-to-date information about everything from Lady Gaga to extrasolar planets…instantly. And it's all free. No subscriptions. And think of the saved shelf space!

The genius of both Google (as well as other search engines) and Wikipedia, is that they each saw potential far beyond where the organization of human knowledge had been for thousands of years. In a single generation it's been as if every person's cerebral cortex has been expanded a billion times. Only you don't have to remember any of it. It's all right there on the Internet, easily found with a few keystrokes. Wikipedia and Google are like having a Vulcan Mind Meld with every person on the planet…or every person with a WiFi connection, anyway. In the words of Mr. Spock, "Fascinating."

All of these examples show what individuals can do by raising their sites, by thinking about how an existing technology or body of knowledge previously accessible to only a small group can be used by billions of ordinary people. These visionaries may not have foreseen the huge impact of their simple ideas, but all of them thought big enough to say, "Let's see."

BIG CREATIVE MESSAGES

Going big also means coming up with and recognizing big creative ideas. And all really big creative ideas are scary. It was risky for Avis to brag about being #2 to Hertz' #1. It was risky for Volkswagen to run its famous "Think Small" ad, highlighting the size and ugliness of its car in the age of road monsters with tailfins. It was risky for tiny Apple to challenge IBM directly in its own lair with its subversive "1984" commercial during the Super Bowl. And it was risky for upstart Wikipedia to challenge traditional academic institutions and their exclusive lock on knowledge.

The one thing that all of these companies had in common was that they started small. They weren't IBM or General Motors or Hertz. They were nobodies at the time, at least in this country. They had relatively small ad budgets and relatively small voices. They were underdogs. But the messages they came up with resonated with the hundreds of millions of fellow underdogs who make up most of the population; people like us.

Volkswagen's "Think Small" was a big message because it got people to rethink the way they not only drove a car, but lived their whole lives. It was in tune, in the 1960s, with a rising popular philosophy toward minimalism and simplification. The 60s' counter-culture movement saw a whole generation rethinking their impact on the environment. Volkswagen's Think Small campaign not only captured that new outlook, but created a car that itself became symbolic of the simplicity movement itself.

"The Computer for the Rest of Us" message for Apple's

Macintosh addressed our entire relationship to technology, not just saying that it was now accessible to ordinary people, but that it *should* be accessible to ordinary people. It was a matter of ethical principle, raising the sites of a marketing campaign to the level of a global, populist cause.

Avis's "We Try Harder" brand message has worked for generations because it speaks to everyone with plain truth. This message is so big, in fact, that it could almost be the brand position of the entire human race. Why did we thrive while the Neanderthals went extinct? We tried harder. And we took risks.

Going big is risky. And it is scary. But it's only by taking big risks with the creativity of your message that you have a chance to make a change in the way people think and act.

In the late 1980s, aerospace company Lockheed, had a big goal: They had targeted 23 key contracts they wanted to win with Congress, including programs for Department of Defense and NASA . These contracts were for everything from the Hubble Space Telescope to the International Space Station, and from the D5 Rocket to the Advanced Tactical Fighter (the F-22). They not only wanted to win contracts for these multi-billion dollar programs, they wanted Congress to keep the programs funded. Of course, Lockheed was already doing all the conventional things to influence these votes; but they were not completely happy with their advertising message, which didn't seem to line up with the loftiness of their goals. They had been running bland ads in the usual aerospace trades with uplifting headlines like "The Future is Now" and "Tomorrow Looks Bright from Up Here." As lofty as the messages sounded, Lockheed felt they were just too predictable. They tended to make people yawn.

So the marketing team at Lockheed and its ad agency decided to take an entirely unexpected and counterintuitive approach to their overall message: history. This ran completely against what everyone expected of aerospace advertising, which was supposed to be focusing on the shiny bright future, not the rusty past. History was for museums, not launch pads. But lessons from history threw an emotional switch inside the brains of the prime movers in Washington and their sense of their own place in history.

The first ad to run was about the Advanced Tactical Fighter, but instead of showing a picture of the jet, it displayed a large detail of the nine-hundred-year-old Bayeux tapestry and the provocative headline, "William the Conqueror and the Advanced Tactical Fighter." The long copy of the ad told the story of the Battle of Hastings in 1066, and how the Normans were able to win that battle because of a recently introduced technological edge: the stirrup. The stirrup, the ad explained, enabled the Norman knights to stay on their horses to fight (Saxon soldiers, without stirrups, fought on foot) and come at the Saxon shield wall like medieval tanks. The copy of the ad pointed out that, by analogy, if the United States did not retain its current technological edge in air superiority by developing the ATF, it could suffer the same fate as the defeated Saxons. Lurid and epic stuff: clashing swords, splintering spears, screaming horses, knights, blood, and the fate of nations in the balance.

Further ads in the advocacy campaign made similar

"moment in history" comparisons: the defeat of Napoleon's fleet at Trafalgar in 1805 with the need for a new communications satellite system now, the Ming Dynasty with the International Space Station, or the ancient Egyptians and Artificial Intelligence. Each ad spanned two pages, feeling like an epic movie. And each analogy was made elegantly and pointedly, as if to say to the reader (i.e. Senator Foghorn, Representative Porkrind, and General Mayhem), "Where is your place in history?"

The Big Message posed by Lockheed was that these programs were historically momentous, that the very survival of civilization was at stake. The message gave the company a position that was unique in the aerospace industry, that Lockheed was the only thing standing between Western Civilization and a new Dark Ages. Lockheed was itself on the white horse, ready to lead the charge into the Saxon shield wall…or outer space.

The ad campaign approached the problem of persuasion from a completely unexpected angle. It appealed to the sense of history in the Members of Congress voting to fund these programs, and to the Pentagon officials responsible for awarding the contracts. It also appealed to Wall Street and the voting public. They didn't need to see pictures of hardware and airplanes, they were seeing themselves at the fulcrum of history.

But the real test for the success of the campaign came in the following three years. Of the original 23 government contracts it had targeted, Lockheed won 19. The creative message was big. It hit the key decision makers right in their egos. And the win for Lockheed was as big as the message.

LIFT YOUR VOICE

The other step in going big is in how loud and often you tell your story. We've seen companies craft highly evocative brand positions, develop innovative products, attend to every detail of putting together a high-potential enterprise, and still flop because they hesitated to put enough into getting the message out. A neat idea alone is not enough to make it take root. You can create a better mousetrap but if you just sit there, expecting the world to beat a path to your door, you're going to wait a long time.

Did you ever run a lemonade stand when you were young? What was your experience? Did you set up the stand in your backyard? In your living room? Of course not; you probably set it up on the sidewalk out front, where it was most visible to the neighbors, right? You put up a sign. You yelled at passing cars. In other words, you advertised. If you were smart enough, you put up a BIG sign, one with letters that could be read from down the block. And if you put the stand at the intersection of the busiest streets in your neighborhood, you probably made even more money. Maybe you roped in some other kids as partners (with minor equity positions) to go up and down the street with their own signs, waving and directing people to your stand. The lesson you were supposed to learn in these early experiences of business—besides making sure sales were greater than the cost of products sold—was that big marketing made all the difference.

Remarkably, grownup businesses don't seem to have learned that lesson. They fret and complain that people should just know, somehow, that they have a better product. They act like the kid who sets up his lemonade stand in the comfort of his mom's backyard.

We had an industrial client who, when the most recent recession started, dutifully cut way back on their advertising budget in an apparent gesture to shareholders that they were being prudent with their spending. During recessions marketing budgets are always slashed first, as if they are a luxury, like teak paneling in the corporate suites. But to the dismay of our client, their main competitor was actually increasing its own ad frequency during this recession. In some of the key trade magazines, the competitor was running six and eight ads an issue. By contrast our client was suddenly absent to its primary audience. The client protested that it wasn't fair. There was a recession on. Didn't those people know? But the competitor saw their chance to make a move, and while our client, who had enjoyed the pole position in the industry for years, pulled off to the side of the road, those other "cheaters" decided to mash down on the pedal and take the lead. Within a year our client had lost its market lead and rumors started circulating that, because no one had seen them advertise in some time, they were going out of business. They weren't, of course (yet), but we refer you to Rule #2, Perception is Reality.

Another cautionary tale comes from the fast food industry. There's a regional chain of Mexican fast food restaurants in the Northwest that has been around since the late 1950s, starting about the same time as rival Taco Bell. Taco Bell, of course, has since become, well, Taco Bell. Our little regional chain is still relatively unknown outside its local customer base.

The reason has not been lack of quality. Franchise owners in the chain are intense about their food, and their existing customers are loyal. But one of the reasons this otherwise estimable chain has not had the success of Taco Bell has been advertising—or lack thereof. The company just doesn't seem to believe in it. They've always done the bare minimum.

As an anecdote to illustrate this, when we were with the chain's ad agency, we went to visit a particularly stubborn franchise owner, a member of the franchise advertising committee, at his own store. He had been the loudest voice against wasting money on advertising and we were advised that if we went to appeal to him personally, we might be able to persuade him.

We stopped by at lunchtime and noticed that his parking lot was empty. He had one, lone customer in the dining room. Across the street, by contrast, his arch-nemesis Taco Bell had a full parking lot and its drive-thru line extended out onto the street. The store owner was not in a good mood when we introduced ourselves. "I know why you're here," he came at us, "You're trying to sell me advertising. Well, let me tell you, my customers don't come here because of the advertising, they come here because of the great food."

We gestured out the window to the crowded Taco Bell across the street and pointed out his empty dining room. "How's that working for you?" It's so rare that life hands you such eloquent visual aids.

"Taco Bell's crap," he said. Needless to say, the meeting did not win him over. He knew what he knew (following Rule #2, Perception is Reality): Advertising didn't work.

We did enjoy, however, a delicious, free burrito lunch combo.

Yes, he was right; Taco Bell's crap. There are, of course, tens of millions of customers who don't think so, but what do they know? However, the relative success of these two companies is not simply that one has invested in advertising and the other has not. It's that the one thought big ("Outside the Bun" as the Taco Bell slogan goes), far beyond its existing customer base, and the other was content to think no further than the customers they had...both of them.

As an example of what can happen when you really lift your voice, take the introduction of the Macintosh in 1984 again (mentioned under Rule #3, Be Creative or Die). Not only did Apple launch its new product with the one-off, highly produced "1984" commercial during the Super Bowl, it followed up later that year with one of the most audacious and lavish media buys in advertising history when it "bought out" the entire November election issue of Newsweek. Every single ad in the magazine was for Macintosh. It was something that had never been done before; the issue had nothing but wall-to-wall election coverage and 39 Mac ads, each one demonstrating the revolutionary idea behind the Macintosh: its accessibility, its innovative graphical interface, the creative things you could do with it. In short, it was "the computer for the rest of us."

The unprecedented scale and audacity of the media buy—reserving an entire issue of one of the leading national news magazines during the priciest time of the year—was itself a media event, and also part of the bigness of the message. This was an earth-shaking new idea and it needed an earth-shaking platform to announce it. The Macintosh mega-campaign was like the trouble-making new kid doing a cannon ball into the pool during adult swim.

The object lesson of these two stories? Think small, stay small. Think big, get big.

SO HOW MUCH IS ENOUGH?

It used to be, when Neanderthals were young, there was a rule of thumb about how much to spend on marketing (a rule of thumb is not to be confused with an Unbreakable Rule): A typical business, thumb said, should invest anywhere between 4-7% of its projected revenues in marketing; four percent if your goal was to hold your own, seven percent if you wanted to aggressively take your competitors to school. Of course, when you're marketing for a non-profit organization, or a political movement, where revenues aren't as important as feet on the street, this 4-7% is more of a "suggestion of thumb" rather than a rule. But regardless of your purpose, to reach people you need to budget some adequate money.

Media planners use a metric called the CPM (for cost per mille). In layman's terms, the CPM is how much it costs to get 1,000 people to see or hear your message. In 2008, according to the eMarketer website, the average CPM for various paid advertising media was a little under six dollars. This ranges from as high as $414 for direct mail down to $2.26 for outdoor advertising. But this is just for conventional media. And there is obviously wide variation depending on the market, the specificity of the audience, the Nielsen ratings of the channels and shows, even the city.

Of course, the new media (social networks, YouTube, and Google) throw in new factors that make the spending formula more complex. The rise of mobile media will further complicate the math. And the creative or entertainment value of the message itself can have a huge effect on how efficient your media dollar is. For something to go viral on the Internet, for instance, it needs to be creative and entertaining enough for people to want to pass it on. It doesn't work to create a dull infomercial and expect it to go viral on its own. This means that, even if you don't spend a dime on traditional media, you usually have to make at least some effort to have something entertaining enough to go viral.

The question, "How much is enough?" is easily answered: Enough to get noticed. But enough doesn't mean just throwing money at media and repeating yourself as often and loudly as possible. In fact, many companies have outspent their rivals in advertising and have still fallen behind. Sometimes you just don't have enough money to spend to compete with General Motors and Apple. So you have to think big to get around that little problem. "Enough" means to think big about your message and about the means you use to get it out there. And thinking big usually means,

"What hasn't been done before?"

The edginess and sheer outrage of a message, its resonance with your audience, even its unexpectedness itself, can do a lot to overcome a budgetary disadvantage. A dull message needs to be repeated many times for it to start to get noticed. An exciting, new message appearing in an unexpected place will be noticed at once.

IT'S AN INVESTMENT, NOT AN EXPENSE

Marketing is not an expense. It's an investment. Plant maintenance is an expense; you don't expect to make any return on custodial services (unless you're a custodial services company). Human Resources is an expense. Phone and Internet services are expenses. Marketing, on the other hand, is not an expense. Marketing is an investment. We can't repeat that enough. Say it out loud to yourself. And, as an investment, you should have an expectation that the return on it will be substantial, even in the hundreds of percent.

One industrial client of ours spent approximately one million dollars on marketing and saw his annual sales jump from around $17 million to $42 million in one year. He did nothing else—no increase in factory capacity, no additional sales force, no new products, no new hires—but he nevertheless enjoyed an astonishing 2500% return on his investment. Of course, there was more to this dramatic success than a simple investment. It wasn't just playing a hunch on a roulette table. There was a lot of expert work. The marketing involved an integrated strategy and an efficient and novel approach to media. And there was a big, creative idea to boost the reach and impact of the message. Much of the investment was in just plain time, work, and creative thinking.

Not all marketing investment is equal. Much depends on the creativity of the message, the cleverness of the media plan, the interconnectedness of the marketing components, the nature of the product and the customers, and a whole lot of technical marketing know-how. Investors on Wall Street who are successful are the ones who do their homework. The same goes for businesses who invest in marketing.

But the biggest hurdle to get over in budgeting for adequate marketing is psychological. Many businesses just can't seem to get over how much marketing costs in time, sweat, brains, and money. They think of it as a needless luxury; something you indulge in during fat times. But, contrary to that misconception, it's in lean times that you should pour it on, if nothing else but to keep from falling behind.

A company that neglects investing in its marketing is doomed, just as if it neglected to invest in productivity, talent, distribution, sales, or any other vital component of its business. Marketing is not a luxury, it is the very thing that pumps the lifeblood of business.

So don't spend a cent on marketing. Invest a bundle in it.

WHEN AND HOW TO MEASURE YOUR RETURN

The biggest complaint about the marketing investment is that it's often infuriatingly hard to measure the return. John Wanamaker, the 19th century department store pioneer, is reputed to have said, "Half the money I spend on advertising is wasted; the trouble is I don't know which half." Unfortunately, this well-known quote is misused by people to throw in the towel and not even try. It is also an excuse to resort only to forms of advertising that can be measured by response rates and click-throughs. Those media are not necessarily more effective, it's only that they can be measured directly. You may have small returns but at least you know what they are. It's like the joke about the drunk searching for his keys under a lamppost: When asked by a friend if that's where he lost them, he says, "No, but the light's better over here." With some forms of advertising, it's not that they're more effective, it's just that the light's better over there.

If you are trying to sell a nifty little invention, say an exercise device that promises to make people look like chiseled Greek gods without having to do any work themselves, (for only $19.99 plus shipping and handling), and you run a direct response commercial on cable TV, you can probably measure the return on that ad directly by how many calls you get while the spot is airing.

Unfortunately, the vast majority of products and services don't have a sales conversion rate like that. People are informed about the product or brand and then, much later, when they find themselves suddenly in need of something just like they saw in that ad months before, they'll go buy it. That's very hard to measure directly. A commercial for Boeing is not likely to get an immediate call at 2:17 AM from an airline needing to order a 787 right away (plus shipping and handling). Nor can you sell food like that. Or clothing. Or cars. Or medical services. Or almost anything when it comes down to it. That's not how people act.

In business, there are so many variables—the state of the economy, the weather, school vacations, the price of gas, the political climate, the phases of the moon—that it's hard to pinpoint a specific marketing campaign as responsible for an increase in sales. Sometimes the increase in sales doesn't come in for weeks or months after the launch of the message, long after the advertiser gives up hope. Sometimes it's even decades.

When Cathey was eight years old and going through the trauma of her parents' divorce, she happened to see an ad for Big Brothers Big Sisters of America on TV. Decades later, feeling the need to reach out to other children at risk, she remembered that ad from her childhood and sought out Big Brothers Big Sisters to volunteer. It was a thirty year lag time between the ad and the conversion. How do you put a metric on that?

Online advertising boasts the advantage of being able to measure click-through as a direct validation of its efficacy. But, as with direct TV, what it's measuring is only the immediate interest of someone who is currently in the mood to buy—a tiny fraction of the potential customer population. It can't measure the overall, long-term impression it makes. You might notice a banner ad on a web page, note the message and file it away in your brain for later, without ever clicking through. Maybe you don't need a new smart phone right now, but in six months, when your service contract runs out, you're likely to remember the cool smart phone you once saw advertised on a banner ad. Whoever is selling you the phone won't know where you heard about it, even if they ask you, because you probably won't remember where you heard about it. How often have you filled out a survey asking, "Where did you hear about us?" The truth is, few of us can recall how we first heard about a brand or a product; we just know about it when we need it. It comes to us from a marketer who has been hitting us from every which way, relentlessly and creatively. And we haven't been keeping track of the one time it finally sank in.

In order to measure the true return of your marketing investment you need to be patient and stand back. Note what your sales or traffic are before you launch a campaign and then what it is after it's been running for a few months. This is just good marketing hygiene. Of course, like everyone else, you're going to want to open the oven to see if the cake has risen yet. But resist that urge. Give it time. You will probably find that sales may be slow at first, but start to build as the effect of your marketing message sinks in. It depends partly on the nature of the thing you're selling, of course; if you're selling hamburgers, you're more likely to see an immediate spike in sales than if you're selling computers. But if your message is big, resonant, and memorable, and if you don't relent, your patience will be rewarded—probably within a quarter or two. Just wait.

Even when marketing yourself personally, you have to be patient. Do everything you need to do. Commit yourself with your image, your message, your networking, and your wooing. But don't lose heart if you don't get the job right away. Plan big and go big. And go for the long haul.

IF YOU TEST IT, TEST IT IN THE REAL WORLD

There is a big temptation, especially in large consumer companies, to test marketing messages and creative ideas in the "laboratory" before "going live." If an idea tests poorly in a focus group, it's easy to kill it. Yet the history of marketing is crowded with successful campaigns that tested poorly, and even more brilliant ideas were choked off in the focus group stage. Nobody honestly knows why an idea dies. Sometimes people in a focus group can talk a great idea to death, or they say they like it but don't know if other people would (suddenly becoming the self-appointed spokesperson for "other people"). Sometimes someone on the client side of the one-way glass is uncomfortable with an idea that scares him (usually a good sign of its power), and is looking for any negative response by the focus group to back up his reticence. Whatever the reasons, these are not relevant to how an idea will play in the real world. The only real test is to run it out there and see.

There is also a temptation to run an ad once or twice and see what kind of response you get before you expand your reach. It's prudent and responsible to test in the marketplace, but make sure the size of the test is large enough that you can make an impression and get adequate feedback. Rule #8 is to Go Big. That means go big on your tests, too. You need to give an idea enough time and enough reach before you can really see how it's sinking in. New Coke took nearly a

year before the backlash kicked in. Most new products take
months of promotion before the public even starts to notice
them, usually long after the advertiser himself gets sick of
the idea. It took us seven whole years, after all, to get to the
moon.

So light that rocket, and stand back.

>DO THIS

Everything you do for your marketing,
do it full out. Do it like you mean it,
or don't even bother.

UNBREAKABLE RULE #9

EVERYTHING IS MARKETING

SMART AND DUMBER

"Here's your dollar. I hope it lasts you a long time because I'm never coming to McDonald's again," said the irate mother as she slapped the bill on the counter. Like many of us parents have done, under the incredible pressure from a whiny child (not that we're proud of it), Karin Kusumakar had taken her daughter into a McDonald's for a Happy Meal. Karin was not wild about McDonald's but she did, at least, appreciate that the Happy Meal had a choice of apples instead of fries, and milk instead of soda. But it seems, on this visit, that they were out of milk. The cashier asked if she wanted to substitute a soda or juice instead and Karin said, "No thanks, we'll just have water."

The cashier generously said, "In that case, I'll just deduct the price of a milk," which was one dollar. Sounded fair. So she rang Karin up, took her money, and went to fill the Happy Box. When she brought it back to the counter, the manager came over and said to the teenage employee, "Just what do you think you're doing? You ring her up for the full price."

"But we didn't have milk, so I deducted the price of it from the Happy Meal," said the minimum-wage employee.

"I don't care. You don't have the authority to give discounts!" he snapped at the poor girl.

Whereupon he turned on Karin and said, bluntly, "You owe another dollar for the drink."

"But you didn't have milk so I didn't get a drink."

"You could have a soda or juice."

"I didn't want a soda or juice, I wanted milk, like it says on the menu."

"I don't care, a Happy Meal is $2.45 and you owe another dollar."

"But it's not a full Happy Meal."

The manager was adamant and not polite about it. He wanted his buck. Karin, just to get out of there, pulled out a dollar bill and smacked it on the counter, and declaimed her telling line about hoping it would last a long time because she wasn't coming back.

Two lessons here about marketing:

LESSON 1: EVERYTHING IS MARKETING

The manager did his marketing exactly wrong. He, as a representative of McDonald's Corporation (it didn't matter if he was just a franchise owner, or a hired employee, the customer didn't know that or care), displayed McDonald's as a greedy, bureaucratic, unhelpful, unlovin'-it, nasty company that openly rips off its customers and bullies its employees. He acted like a self-destructive moron. He managed to chase away a potential regular customer for life (and let's face it, nearly every parent of kids is a potential regular customer), depriving his company of thousands of dollars in future revenue.

But wait, there's more: He also created an anti-McDonald's partisan who would tell her story to scores of other people, who would, in turn, tell it to scores of others, and so on. We ourselves are participating in this time-honored ritual by passing on this anecdote to the dozens of people who may read this book. This is a multiplier that converts the revenue lost to hundreds of thousands, certainly more than the salary of the manager.

Finally, he evoked the wrong emotion in a customer: anger.

LESSON 2: EVERYTHING IS MARKETING

The teenage employee did her marketing exactly right. She demonstrated creativity (Rule #3) by reducing the cost of the Happy Meal by the price of the missing milk. She demonstrated love for the customer (Rule #6) by making up for the customer's disappointment that they didn't have milk. She proved, by her empathy for the customer, the company's stated values as a family-friendly restaurant, thereby following Rule #2, Perception is Reality. She demonstrated commitment by risking her job, which is going big (Rule #8) in a tangible way. Of course, she probably wasn't aware she was doing these things; she was just trying to make a customer happy and get through her shift.

But, let's face it, that reclaimed dollar potentially ended up costing McDonald's millions not sold.

WHEN DOES IT STOP?

Marketing never stops. Even after you've made the sale, your marketing goes on. Now you have a more intimate relationship with your customer because she has your product in her life. She's in a position to come back for more, or to recommend you to her friends. So you can't let up.

It gets worse. Say you've lost a customer. You're still not off the hook for marketing. How you respond to him is important to your overall message. Unhappy customers give you an opportunity to win them back for life, depending on how you handle their complaints. Even if winning them back is not possible (let's face it, some people would just rather be mad), the way you deal with them sends a message to any witnesses, whether they are other customers, your own employees, or just passersby. And in this age of Angie's List, online reviews, and Facebook, your engagement with the public is more visible than ever. It may feel good in the spirit of the moment to shout, "Same to you, pal!" as a pissed-off customer storms out the metaphorical door, but keep that understandable (and probably justifiable) outburst to yourself. How you respond under attack is also a marketing message. Other people are noticing.

It's like marriage after dating. During the courtship period, both people are marketing themselves to each other in the best possible light. They are attentive to personal hygiene, treat each other with the utmost affection and courtesy, and instinctively follow all the other eight rules of marketing. They are eager to make the sale. But then, after the wedding, the marketing behavior often gets neglected. Courtesy and affection fade, they stop laughing at each other's jokes, and... what's that smell? The next thing you know, they start looking for another customer, another sale. As divorced couples will attest, the turnover costs are enormous, as are the new customer acquisition costs.

We can go even further: The way two people treat each other during a breakup will also affect how they relate to all of their community thereafter. As with the ugly customer you show the door, the spouse you are seeing out still has an influence on everyone else in your life. And everyone else in your life takes note of how you behave during this stressful time. Friends and family may stay loyal, but how you act forever alters their perception of you (see Rule #2, Perception is Reality). You may have a good excuse for behaving badly during a breakup, but the fact that you did is a bell that can never be unrung. Everyone hears it, and keeps hearing it.

Whether in personal relationships or business, if you can remember that the marketing never quits, your customers will stay loyal. They can even bring you more customers. Or at least a long, happy relationship. (Be sure to look for our upcoming book, *The Unbreakable Rules of Marriage*)

MARKETING DOWN TO YOUR BONES

This is the Unbreakable Rule that many people have the hardest time understanding: Everything you do is marketing. Because of the mindset that most people have about marketing—that it is a separate function of business involving ads, sales brochures, and websites—it is hard to grasp that these are just part of it. Your entire enterprise is a marketing vehicle. It just takes a shift in perspective to see the whole.

Everything that influences how someone will think of your business, your organization, your product, even yourself, is marketing. Marketing isn't some separate little function they do on the 17th floor of corporate headquarters. It isn't just the advertising or the promotions or the trade shows you have to attend every year. It's even in the little, seemingly insignificant things you do that affects what people think of you, from your multimillion-dollar, globally deployed ad campaign right down to the way your receptionist answers the phone. It includes the quality and design of your products. It's in how you treat your employees. But on a personal level it even includes something as seemingly trivial as your haircut or how high you wear your pants.

We are marketing animals.

Have you ever been in a conversation with a person who refuses to look you in the eye? Where are his eyes looking? What do you think of that person? Is he just shy? Is he hiding something? Can you trust him? Well, all of that eye-shifting is part of his own personal marketing, whether he's conscious of it or not. Even the most subtle and fleeting gestures of the eyes or the muscles of the face can tell you when someone is lying, or thinking about something else, or really connecting with you. It's marketing at work on the most basic level: personal. We are constantly engaged in marketing behavior even when we're not aware of it.

Here's another example of personal marketing: Imagine having lunch with someone you've just met. During the meal he is extremely attentive to you, the soul of gentility and warmth. But you notice that he's short with the waitress, treating her like a despised servant. To you he's genuine, kind, respectful, and attentive; to this other person who has no value to him (aside from the obvious risk of insulting someone who has access to his food outside of his view) he's a jerk. What do you think of this person in general; nice to you, nasty to the "little people"? Can you trust him not to treat you like that waitress when he no longer needs you? Isn't he two-faced? Well, that's how he markets himself. His personal brand is "Jerk." He isn't self-aware enough to notice it; he's too close to himself. But his every action markets that personal brand message: "I'm a jerk."

On the other hand, having lunch with someone who is as genuinely kind and respectful to the waiter as he is to you is marketing himself as a considerate person. You can trust him. His personal brand is "Great Guy." You are more likely to want to spend time with him. If he were a product you'd feel better about buying him. His message to you, to the waiter, to his dog, to everyone who knows him is, "I'm a great guy." But being a great guy, he would never say that about himself. He just uses his every action to market himself that way.

These interpersonal signals are also a good way to judge a company's character. In short, how do they treat their employees?

Take this principle to your own experience as a customer.

Have you gone to a store and noticed the employees openly complaining to each other about their boss, or the company in general? Or even if they are not openly complaining, you can still pick up on unhappiness in the workplace. It's infectious. Most people are generally empathetic to the plight of other human beings, so if we notice those employees are unhappy, we tend to feel unhappy ourselves. They are the face of the company, and it's not a happy face. You'll tend to avoid going back to that store—unless, of course it's the only store within a fifty mile radius.

The opposite experience is a store where all of the employees seem happy; they joke with the customers and each other, they appear to like being at work, and they're glad to see you. You like going to that place because you tend to feel as happy as the employees. Starbucks and Disney have applied and cultivated this organic marketing for years. They know that the best ad for their brand is the way their customers are treated by their employees. And to get that effect, they know they have to treat their employees well in turn. It's paying it forward (see Rule #6, Give Love to Get Love).

You can't force employees to be happy for your customers. That usually backfires. You've probably seen promotions in retail establishments that guarantee a smile or your order is free. All that does is put pressure on the poor clerk to pretend to be happy, or else. And everyone can spot a forced smile. We're all experts at reading the truth in faces. A promotion like this says to the customer, "We bully our employees for you." Unless their customers are sadists, this is not the brand message a company probably wants to send. Nor can you control the banter (good or bad) that happens behind the counter or on Facebook. Bad vibes seep out.

This is the point: Whether you realize it or not, you are constantly marketing in everything you do. It's in your bones. If you are conscious of it, you can control the impression you make, for yourself personally and your business. If you aren't conscious of it, you're still marketing, and that marketing may be negative.

BE AWARE, BE SELF-AWARE

Have you ever had the unnerving experience of watching yourself in a candid video? Are you shocked by what you see? Do you ever want to reach into the screen and throttle that imposter for misrepresenting you? This is what happens when you are not aware of how you come across. Like everybody, we all have this image of ourselves in our heads that is probably not aligned with the same perception others have of us. We may, for instance, think we're a good listener and then see, in that incriminating party video, that we hog the conversation. Our personal marketing story is the person we want to be. But our personal marketing behavior may not support that story outside the confines of our skulls. There's a disconnect between internal belief and reality, or at least perceived reality. The second Unbreakable Rule, Perception is Reality, even works on ourselves.

Huge corporations are also vulnerable to this kind of self-deception. Their advertising may brag about how much they care, how great their customer service is, or how they are committed to quality, but the perception on the other side of the counter may be the opposite. In fact, so common is this corporate self-deception that we, as consumers, have become cynical about the self-congratulatory claims of customer service, quality, and caring. We almost instinctively know that if a company's slogan is "We Care," what they really mean is "We Got Nuthin'."

We are all aware of companies who give mere lip service to vague marketing claims. They are, unfortunately, more common than smart, self-aware businesses. Smart businesses try to go beyond lip service by hiring market research firms to find out what people really think of them, versus what they say about themselves. Really smart businesses will listen to that feedback. They'll start fleshing out the main marketing message (say "customer service") onto every detail of their business. If their marketing message is "attention to detail," for example, they'll apply that to all aspects of their operations, from product design to factory to sales to shipping to customer service. And all of that falls under marketing.

FedEx has been a good example of that principle of self-awareness. FedEx is all about time. Their first, memorable advertising slogan (ironically, also one of the longest in advertising history) was "When it absolutely, positively has to be there overnight." That tagline expressed the sole criterion for the customer to rate FedEx; not customer service, not smiling truck drivers, not greatest volume, not more ways to ship, not even most the economical way to ship... just the fastest. Everything about FedEx, from its customer service to its logistical models, has to do with fulfilling that one objective. Time is the message. This marketing approach has been so successful that the very term "FedEx" has become a generic verb to ship something to someone as fast as possible (the same way that the term "Kleenex" has been used as a common term for tissue and "Google" has been used as a common term for searching online).

In an elegant example of free-product placement, Tom Hanks, in the 2000 movie, *Cast Away*, plays a FedEx executive who passionately explains this single-minded obsession with on-time delivery, "Time rules over us without mercy, not caring if we're healthy or ill….we live or we die by the clock." The entire movie, in fact, is like a commercial for FedEx, with a little human drama thrown into the mix for entertainment. Though FedEx paid nothing for its prominent placement in the film (and was, reportedly, a little nervous about a screenplay involving the crash of a FedEx plane), the upshot was that the filmmakers so understood this pervasive marketing message of the company as to make it the driving irony of the screenplay: a man obsessed with being on time unexpectedly made late by several years. Even so, in the outcome, even when they make a mistake, FedEx comes out looking like the company who you want shipping your packages.

When filmmakers that don't even work for you take your marketing message and turn out a blockbuster movie about that message, that's marketing with a vengeance.

Marketing lives in every fiber of your being. You need to be conscious of how every aspect of your business affects that message; does it reinforce it or does it contradict it?

If your marketing message is about customer service, do you reward your employees who display innovation and creativity to extend that service? Or do you punish employees who don't follow the rules, like the McDonald's manager berating his employee, "You don't have the authority to give discounts!"? If your company has branded itself around quality, do you reward factory workers who pull the stop chain when they discover defects coming down the line? Or are they punished for interrupting the output? Remember, word gets out quickly among your employees how to get rewarded and how to get in trouble. And people will naturally stay well away from what gets them in trouble.

Marketing is the distillation of all aspects of your business. Let's say a hypothetical office products retailer runs an ad campaign that proudly claims:

"NO HASSLE RETURN POLICY!"

This policy is not only announced in TV and radio ads, it's in newspaper inserts, it's emblazoned on gigantic banners on the outside and inside of the store, and on shelf-talkers. It's everywhere, even on the bottom of cash register receipts. In smaller print it explains, "If you have a problem with any of our products in the next year, don't send it to the manufacturer, just bring it back to any of our stores and we'll give you a brand new one. No hassles!" Sounds pretty clear.

Now let's say a customer of this store has a problem

with…oh…say a Bluetooth headset. The thing just doesn't connect to his mobile device, even after he repeatedly follows the exact instructions. The customer, remembering the marketing message of "NO HASSLE RETURNS" takes the thing back. He's got all the receipts, paperwork, original packaging, even down to the little plastic baggies. When he explains to the clerk that he wants to return it, the hassle begins. It's explained back to him that he needs to send the product to the original manufacturer (even though the policy on the receipt specifically says that isn't necessary) and it should take eight to ten weeks to receive a replacement.

The customer is now mad. It's already been a hassle enough that the product he bought in good faith doesn't work. It's been a further hassle that he's had to get back in his car and drive down to the store to return it. Now he's being told of a mouse-type clause explaining the policy doesn't apply to products still covered by original factory warranty.

He walks out of the store with his useless "new" device and aware of a completely different marketing message than the one proclaimed by the store's advertising, namely:

"WE'RE BIG FAT LIARS!"

This is how a disconnect between your promise or self-image and your actual practice can derail your marketing. Before you launch a new ad campaign, make absolutely sure that every detail of your company can back up the promise. And make doubly sure that your boots on the ground, the employees that have to deliver on the thing promised, know what's expected of them. If you put them in the position of having to weasel through the fine print with your customers, you're going to make everybody unhappy: employees, customers, and eventually shareholders. In other words, don't make promises you can't keep.

Contrast this disconnected marketing approach with the famous one of Nordstrom, known widely (even in regions where no Nordstrom stores exist) for its real hassle-free return policy. As we previously pointed out, Nordstrom never brags about this, never even advertises it. It's a brand position that has seeped into the popular culture through anecdotes (some of them dubious, like the guy who returned tires to Nordstrom—which is actually a true story). Everyone seems to know of Nordstrom's brand promise, somehow. The reason they know it is because the marketing is done person-to-person, right on the floor. Nordstrom sales associates are encouraged to make the return so easy because each time they do it, they reinforce that customer bond. Also, experience has shown that people who come in to return something to Nordstrom frequently spend more money before they leave.

So many people have had satisfying experiences from Nordstrom that their standard of customer service has become a benchmark for the entire retail culture, like FedEx becoming synonymous with on-time delivery, or Kleenex for tissues, or Coke for a soft drink. When this happens, when the brand name itself stands as the quintessential noun or verb of the category, then you have achieved marketing nirvana. It may drive the trademark attorneys crazy, but the marketing people love it. Every time someone uses the phrase, "Google it," or "Have you got a Kleenex?" or "FedEx it to me" they are running a little ad for Google, Kleenex, and FedEx.

WE ARE SWIMMING IN MARKETING

Marketing is all around us. It is so pervasive that our brains, just to control the hurricane of input, have become quite good at filtering it. We've come to see marketing only in ads. But the ads are only the most obvious form of marketing, so it's easy to ignore them. What we are probably not aware of, because the filtering is on automatic, is what's below the surface of messaging. For every ad we ignore, there are probably dozens of other, more subtle marketing signals hiding in plain sight. This is a neurobiological function our brains perform out of sheer self-preservation. We've evolved to pay attention not only to what's different in our environment, but also to what's necessary for survival. If we had to process every single piece of input, figuring out an appropriate response and filing it away, we'd quickly fry our neurons. There's even a clinical disorder for people who have trouble filtering sensory input: Adult Sensory Processing Disorder (ASPD). But most people with well-functioning brains can only pay attention to the incoming messages that are of immediate interest, filtering out everything else before it even reaches consciousness. It's like the brain has a spam filter. Otherwise, our sensory environment is a cacophony of marketing background radiation.

You see car ads constantly, for instance. But you are only interested in them when you are actually shopping for a car, or when your current clunker is back in the shop again. So your brain can turn on and off the attention to the whole category of car marketing depending on your need.

If you are 18, you are much less likely to pay attention to retirement planning and financial product commercials than if you are 58. This is because the subject matter is suddenly more relevant when the issue is more personally immediate. The interest level turns on or off depending on how foreground the need or desire is in your life at the time.

You eat every day. So the decision about what to eat for lunch comes up much more frequently than buying a new car, or tires, or car insurance. But ads that make you hungry for that juicy burger are much more effective if you notice them at 11:30 AM than at 11:30 PM—unless of course, you're a teenage boy. Timing, whether during the day or over the span of your life, is the secret not just to comedy, but to marketing. You're the gatekeeper, deciding what gets in and when. But you are also at the beck and call of your needs.

Regardless of this automatic filtering, the marketing background radiation is always there, whether you pay attention to it or not. You may not be conscious of the marketing in the feel of a Mac laptop. Its design, its materials, even the tactile sensation of the keys and the texture of the cover are all consciously devised to elicit a comforting response from owners and even those just "browsing" in the Apple Store. The sound of the pings on an iPad or iPhone are designed with the same, emotional stimulation in mind. During the Pixar movie, *Wall-E*, when the little robot reboots, the familiar Mac gong sound prompted a giggle of recognition—but also reassurance—from the Mac owners in the audience. Even a post-apocalyptic future will have Apple.

Driving down the street, every car we pass is itself a marketing message. Every store sign, every logo on every product in our house is an ad. Even our clothing has become advertising, with our chests and behinds as billboards for slogans and logos. When we go into a supermarket to get some milk, we enter such a dense field of marketing signals that our brain is plowing through thousands of them before we even get back to the dairy section (there's a reason they put staples like milk and eggs at the back of a store). The uniforms of the employees are marketing; the attitude of the clerks is marketing; and the grocery baskets are vehicles for little ads. Even our garbage itself is a salad of marketing messages, all winking at us.

When a Harley Davidson goes by, that rumbling growl you feel from the sidewalk through your feet up into your guts: Marketing.

Ever drive by a bakery and notice that baked bread smell in the air? Marketing.

Ever watch a Congressional hearing? It's all marketing; marketing by the politicians to their constituents, marketing on the other side by the poor bastards (or lucky ducks, depending on the circumstances) hauled in (or invited) to testify.

Do you watch the news on TV? Not only are news

channels constantly streaming self-promotional messages at us, they've even buried their brand into the very content of the news itself. You are never in doubt for one second about who is bringing you this breaking story. The screen is broken up into several segments of scrolling type, inset video frames, logos, and graphics so that you don't know where to look next. Watching the news today is like drinking from a fire hose.

To be fully conscious every waking moment of the sheer size of the marketing sea we are swimming in would cause a cerebral meltdown. So we just ignore most of it. On some level we are still taking it in on what they used to call a subliminal channel. We are more responsive to the marketing messages that may appeal to us (like the feel of a Mac laptop), but 99% of them go directly to the spam folder in our brains.

About the only way we can escape the sea of marketing, it would seem, would be to get away from civilization and get out into nature.

But we'd be wrong.

MARKETING IS IN OUR GENES

Nature is full of examples of marketing. Flowers market to bees by their color (often ultraviolet) and scent. Male birds market to females with their song, their plumage, and sometimes by silly dances (well, maybe not silly to the birds). Lions market to lionesses by their manes (the blacker the better, as studies have shown). The black and yellow banding you see on wasps, bees, snakes, and some frogs markets the message "danger" to would-be predators. We even use that color pattern in our own culture to advertise danger. Ants send marketing messages about food and danger by leaving pheromone markers. Deep sea creatures advertise for mates by bioluminescent patterns. Everywhere you look, smell, hear, and feel in nature you are experiencing marketing. Nearly every life form, in fact, uses marketing behavior to reproduce, eat, and survive. Marketing, in other words, is a fact of life.

So to turn our noses up at marketing and its intrusion into our lives as though it was a new thing in our culture is to ignore the fact that it's always been with us, for at least 542 million years. It is in our very genes.

You have to wonder on a spring morning in the country, if all the cacophony of noisy birds advertising their presence doesn't somehow irritate those very birds who are trying themselves to get noticed. Do they wish, like we do when we are bombarded by a torrent of marketing messages, that all of those other birds would just shut up so they can get their own message out?

Marketing is fundamental to life. To believe that marketing our businesses is one of those discretionary expenditures we can cut in tough economic times is nuts. It would be as foolish for a company to cut back on its marketing activity as it would be for a bird to stop singing to attract a mate, or a plant to stop flowering to attract bees, or an elk to do without growing an impressive rack of antlers one year. While all of these decisions would definitely save energy, they would also reduce the chances of survival. To the creatures who cut their "marketing budgets", there would be no next generation. So too with businesses.

Marketing, therefore, is everywhere and in everything you do, whether on a business level, a political level, a social level, a personal level, or even a biological level. It is the very engine of life. When you are aware of this, and how you are constantly in the process of marketing, you are better able to control the impression you want to make on customers, employees, investors, potential mates, everyone. Being conscious of it allows you to be in a better position to control the impression you make. And that, in turn, gives you more control over your own fate.

YES, THIS IS MARKETING, TOO!

What follows are some examples of things that you may not think of as marketing. We're not here to tell you how to filter them out; you're already an expert at that. We just want you to be aware of them in your own marketing. It's not an exhaustive list. It's merely intended to get you in the habit of thinking about how everything you do sends a message.

E-MAIL FORMATS

Something as innocuous as the format of your e-mail can make a big impression about your business.

Do you sign off with the same signature every time? Do you use your company logo? Your title? Do you end with, "Sincerely" or "Best" or more informally, like "Later, potater"? Do you greet the addressee formally, "Dear Ms. McGillicutty," less formally, "Hey, Lucy," or do you just jump in without any salutation?

Do you get to the point quickly, respecting the recipient's time? Or do you chew the fat with platitudes like "Your business is important to us..."?

Do you break your e-mail into bullet points for easy reference if there are several points to be made?

Is the point of the e-mail in the subject line, so the person knows whether to open it or not? Or, if it's pertinent to an ongoing issue, to help them find it again among the hundreds of other e-mails they get every day?

Do you check for typos and grammatical errors before you send? Or do you solely rely on the squiggly red line to proof your e-mails? Most people think that this is good enough, somehow believing that any form of electronic communication is exempt from good grammar and spelling. But if you want people—particularly business associates and especially customers—to take you seriously, it's just as important to proofread your own e-mail before you hit the irrevocable "send" button. Their impression of you may depend on it (though they'd never tell you they thought you were an illiterate boob).

When you "Reply All", are you sure that "All" want to see your reply?

Do the e-mails from various people in your company all look like they come from the same organization? Or is there a smorgasbord of logos, title formats, fonts, and signatures? If you are trying to impress your clients that you are a well-run enterprise, having a wide variety of logos and formats going out in your name doesn't exactly reinforce that impression. You won't seem like a legitimate organization. You may just look like a Nigerian 419 scam.

Do you tend to type your e-mails in all caps? This can be annoying to some readers because all caps are harder to read, and it also means that you're yelling. Or do you pretend you're e.e. cummings and don't bother capping anything at all? Or punctuating?

How quickly do you reply to e-mails? If you're asked a question and don't immediately know the answer, do you at least ping the person back to let them know you don't know yet but are finding out? Do you follow through? Little things like failing to acknowledge an e-mail itself sends a not-so-subtle message back. Even no answer is an answer. But don't answer while you're driving or operating heavy machinery. Be safe. Just don't forget to answer soon.

There are no right or wrong ways to format your personal or company e-mails. But you should think about how they come across. They are little ads themselves. And little details like spelling, format, tone of voice, even excessive use of emoticons can convey an impression you may not have intended.

ANSWER THE PHONE!

Have you ever called a business and the person on the other end just says, "Hullo?" This probably doesn't happen that much. But something as simple as how you answer the phone sends a marketing message. We once worked for an ad agency whose poor receptionist was required to answer the phone with a greeting script so long that customers started complaining to her bosses that they'd rather just have a direct line to them.

And how do you answer your own phone? In this day of caller ID it's even possible to see whether or not the caller is a customer, known vendor, or your mom. It shouldn't matter, though. Unless your brand position is Jerk, wouldn't you want to answer the call as if you'd been waiting for that person to call you all day? It's another opportunity to apply Rule #6, Give Love to Get Love.

As with e-mails, though, it's also important to respect the time of the person calling. It's usually sufficient, if it's a call into the main office line, for the operator to just state the name of the company and their first name. But if it's to your direct line, shouldn't you at least say your own name when you answer? Little things like this can convey an impression of a well-run business, just as phone discourtesy can give the opposite impression. If the way you and your employees answer the phone is sloppy, unprofessional, or inappropriate, that's your real brand message: sloppy, unprofessional and inappropriate. It's a negative ad, even though all you've done is answer the phone.

DRESS CODES

"What?! You gonna tell me how to dress now?"

No, but we are going to tell you that how you and your employees dress and present themselves physically is also an ad for your company. If you want people to think you are a slovenly, amateurish, fly-by-night company about to go out of business at the end of the month, then by all means, dress that way. Just be deliberate about it.

Look at Best Buy. Everybody in there is wearing a uniform. It may be nothing more than a polo shirt and khaki pants, but it's still a uniform. And every uniform is clean and pressed. The people are well-groomed. Even over at the aptly named Geek Squad desk at Best Buy, the uniform fits the image of the geek culture: white short-sleeved shirt, black tie. But even for geeks, they are well-dressed geeks. So in talking to them about the dumb thing you did to your laptop when you decided to click on the suspicious e-mail attachment from Uzbekistan, you feel like they know what they're doing, and that's reassuring. They're proud of their professionalism; proud to be good enough to be on the Geek Squad.

Contrast that with a competing big-box electronics chain (which shall remain nameless, but you probably know who we're talking about), in which the employees are dressed similarly to the Geek Squad, but the shirts are wrinkled, dingy, and ill-fitting, matching the attitudes of the employees. The "sales associates" are disdainful of you and seem to be resentful that they have work with a bunch of idiots who don't know how to run their own computers. The minute you enter this store you just want to get to the bin that has the thingamabob you need and get out as fast as possible...through the gauntlet of impulse Baby Ruth Bars and beef jerky in the checkout chute.

Both Best Buy and UnName have security (shrinkage is high in consumer electronics), but at the former, the security person greets you pleasantly and then thanks you pleasantly as you leave. At UnName, you feel like you're lucky they let you in and lucky to get out. And heaven help you if you need help, even though UnName employs around 400 people per store (as of 2009) while Best Buy averages only about 140 per store. It's not hard to find a helpful, pleasant employee at the latter, while you wonder where everybody is at the former.

Which company do you think is kicking the other's butt? While UnName had almost a decade head start on its competitor, Best Buy has grown to more than 25 times UnName's revenue, with 180,000 employees in stores on three continents. The crisp uniforms and pleasant employees could have a little to do with that growth. Though there are probably a lot of other factors, every single one contributes to their success, even something as seemingly insignificant as a clean shirt.

PAINT YOUR WAGON

Even the color of your product can have an effect on your marketing. You might think that you just make an industrial machine, so what difference does the color make? Paint it grey, for all you care. But John Deere and Caterpillar both make industrial machines. And their equipment can be spotted from space, they're so well branded by their respective green and yellow brand colors.

If you're an engineer or an industrial customer, you may wince at the idea that the mere color of a piece of equipment would affect your opinion of it. But it does. It's not that you choose it because of its color, but a familiar, consistent color (Rule #1, Consistency Beats Ability) comes to stand as a shortcut to the feelings of confidence you have in that product. Even a company like Agilent Technologies, that makes things like signal generators and mass spectrometers, are very careful about the physical appearance of their instruments. They sweat details down to the bezel on the face plate, the color of the casing, and the feel of the buttons. They recognize that these things subconsciously remind their customers of the reliability of their equipment. These things also remind their customers that Agilent is all about precision and reproducible results. If its products are precise and consistent looking, by extension so must be the data they put out.

So even though you make a product whose performance doesn't depend on what color it is, be deliberate about the color anyway. Think about what it looks like, feels like, sounds like (the Mac start-up gong and the Harley rumble), tastes like, even smells like (that peculiar BMW new-car smell). And attend to every detail. Because even those seemingly inconsequential, sensory attributes communicate the message you want to get across. They help cement the bond with your customer.

SMALL IS BIG

You need to attend to every detail of your marketing, even if it doesn't at first seem like marketing. It doesn't matter how small the detail is. You could be a one-person business—a handyman, say—and the crispness of your attire, the neatness of your tools, even the professional look of your work order form, all reinforce the trust and confidence your customers want to have in you. If you show up at their house reeking of B.O., three inches of butt crack on parade, tools disorganized and dirty, and in a truck without any visible logo, they're not going to be filled with confidence that you can do the job.

Recently Jeff had to have his septic tank emptied. The man who came to do it drove up in a sparkling bright tanker truck. Every detail of the truck was clean and polished; even the tank was chromed, making it look incongruously like a sanitized milk truck instead of what it was really hauling (don't want to think about that). Both the driver (the owner of the company) and his assistant (his son) wore clean, white jumpsuits. Jeff was impressed and commented on it.

The septic tank emptier explained that the residential septic industry was a very competitive business (one wonders why) and that it was important that everything,—his truck, his uniform, even the equipment he used—was all polished and about as far from what you'd expect a scum sucker would look like. The service he provided was something that people didn't want to think about. His customers didn't even want to shake his hand. So it was important that the visual impression they had when he arrived took their minds as far away from what he was there to do as possible.

Here was a brilliant marketer, even though it was just him, his son, and his sparkling truck. He had a thriving business pumping gawdawful muck out of people's backyards, and he understood that he had to make his customers comfortable. The whole experience was made surprisingly pleasant, making you want to refer him to others, recommend him on Angie's List, and call him back.

He may be a two-man business, but he gets marketing.

>DO THIS

Every little thing you do influences
how people think of you. Sweat the
small stuff and the big stuff will follow.

THE ½ RULE

KNOW THE RULES AND KNOW WHEN TO BREAK THEM

PAY THE MAN AND MOVE ON

What would you do if you had to pay a fine of $5,000 each time you wore a pair of red sneakers? Pay the fine, of course.

In 1985 Nike signed a deal with a promising but young rookie named Michael Jordan to endorse their newly-designed basketball shoe. NBA regulation dress codes stated that players had to wear white shoes. So when Jordan came out wearing his flashy red and black Nikes, the NBA's delicate, country club sensibilities were offended. They banned the shoes from future games, and threatened to fine Jordan $5,000 if he wore anything but white shoes on the court again.

Somebody at Nike evidently made a marketing calculation that even if they paid Jordan's fines for every game he wore the offending shoes, the resulting exposure would still be far less than the media cost of a single NBA playoff commercial. So Jordan, who went on to become possibly the greatest basketball player of all time, kept wearing the shoes, with Nike paying his fines to the persnickety NBA. The Air Jordan and its descendants subsequently became the most successful line of athletic shoes ever sold.

Nike broke the rules. They were bad. They calculated the costs and weighed them against the huge potential gains. To them it wasn't a fine; it was a marketing investment that paid off phenomenally. So they were good to be bad.

You've just read about the 9 Unbreakable Rules of Marketing. But if you're like a lot of people, the first thing you think of when someone gives you an unbreakable rule is to figure out how to break it. And, admit it, you've been thinking about that the entire time you've read this book.

Just as Nike calculated its cost/benefit of breaking the NBA's medieval sumptuary laws, whenever you contemplate the breaking of one of the 9 Unbreakable Rules of Marketing, you should also think about the cost/benefit. It's going to be a rare occasion when breaking one of the rules will reap more rewards than following it. So you'd better have a good reason. And a good reason isn't just because it's convenient, or that they are too hard to follow.

When, then, can you break an Unbreakable Rule?

LET'S TAKE RULE #1, "CONSISTENCY BEATS ABILITY"

This is probably the rule that's easiest to think of breaking. One reason to ignore it is that your company's message has, over the years, become irrelevant and it's time to refresh your brand. Then, obviously, you'd want to break the consistency rule. But first make sure that your brand and your message have really become irrelevant or stale. Be honest with yourself; becoming personally bored with a brand position is not a reason to change it. In fact, experience has shown that an advertiser becomes tired of their own advertising long before the public is even aware of it. Can you imagine Avis changing their promise, "We try harder" just because they've had it for fifty years? It's still a strong position. It still rings true and is a viable philosophy to live by. So changing it, say, to "The Best Value in Rent-a-Cars" would announce that Avis no longer thinks it matters to try harder.

When you do change a brand message, it's also advisable to try to keep a bridge to the past, just so you don't break that bond you had with your audience. Coke has changed its packaging, tagline, and advertising over the years; often subtly. But each time it has made sure there was continuity. When the "It's the real thing" became "Coke is it" became "Always," each slogan reminded its customers that the authenticity of Coke is timeless. And when FedEx changed its tagline from "When it absolutely, positively has to be there overnight" to "The world on time" they kept the same message, just a little shorter—if a little duller.

WHEN TO BREAK RULE #2, "PERCEPTION IS REALITY"

Rule #2 isn't a rule so much you can't break as one you can't ignore. Even if you know that the perception people have of you is false (if they only knew you or your company like you do), the fact remains that their perceptions are their realities and you can't ignore that.

But if they have a negative perception, that doesn't mean

you have to accept it and bow your head in shame. Don't turn an unfair perception into a self-fulfilling prophecy. Do whatever it takes to change it.

Of course it's wise to be aware of any negative perceptions, but temporarily put them aside and get down to what you know is really true about yourself. Don't try to be something you aren't just to please a cranky audience. The public will see right through that sham and add "self-deluding phony" to their list of opinions about you.

And don't try to change those negative perceptions by arguing with them. The trouble with the "Not Your Father's Oldsmobile" type of argument is that it reminds people that it *is* your father's Oldsmobile and you're just in denial. When Nixon said, "I'm not a crook," many people started wondering if he wasn't a crook.

Instead, do like Old Spice did when they revived their old brand of aftershave. Instead of denying that they were your father's aftershave, they took the same logo, the same bottle, the same old package, even the same old jingle that your father (and his father) loved and applied a very entertaining twist with "The Man Your Man Could Smell Like" campaign. They embraced the old perception and turned its camp into something new and hip through the power of creativity.

Taking on a negative perception of an old brand also has the effect of pumping up the morale of the troops. A bad, embarrassing, or stodgy public perception of a company is probably also held by its own employees. Often, changing a public perception starts with working on the internal perception. If your employees are excited about working for you, that's going to communicate to the outside world. So get your own house in order first.

Even though the public owns its perception of you, you can still actively try to influence that perception. That's not ignoring Rule #2, it's bending it to your will.

WHEN TO BREAK RULE #3, "BE CREATIVE OR DIE"

Frankly, we can't think of a time when you wouldn't need to be creative. You may be pressured by forces in your organization (like a timid boss) not to be creative because, well, creativity is often scary. But timidity is not a good enough reason to break this rule. It may be a good reason to keep your job, though…at least for a short time. But it won't help your marketing.

You might think that the subject matter would preclude creativity in some cases. Say you were advertising for a funeral home. Clearly, a humorous solution would probably be inappropriate (though, as we pointed out earlier, we ran a very successful, humorous, TV campaign for Forest Lawn Mortuaries), but remember that creativity doesn't just mean being funny; it means finding an emotionally evocative way to get through to people. So a highly creative way to get people to think about funeral homes might be to touch them in a way that hadn't been thought of before. It doesn't have to be funny. It can also be moving in other ways.

It's often been said that creativity has no place in direct marketing—or "yell-and-sell", as the practitioners of that niche sometimes refer to it. There seems to be an almost unwritten rule, or at least a tradition, that an infomercial must be tedious and information-rich. That's probably why so many infomercials are so dreadfully dull that you find yourself getting up to make a sandwich when they come on. But there is no reason an infomercial can't be creative. Much as we tried, we couldn't find any constitutional prohibition against it. Even "long form" infomercials (30 minutes or more), should be creative. Obviously, you wouldn't use the same techniques you would use on a 30 second commercial, but it should be entertaining nonetheless. Remember, creativity's purpose is to emotionally engage your audience, not put them to sleep. So even in the traditionally boring world of direct marketing, there is no institutional reason to break the creativity rule.

Breaking the third rule is a hard one. About the only time we can conceive of doing it is when you want your company and its brand to come across as a staid, dull, innovation-free institution that isn't going to scare its customers or shareholders. But even managing that image requires some deft creativity.

So, try as we did to think of a time when you could break this rule, we couldn't come up with any instances. If any come to you, let us know.

WHEN TO BREAK RULE #4, "THE MEDIUM IS NOT THE MESSAGE"

To break this rule would be to give priority to the delivery vehicle over the message. But there are many instances when the two are mutually supportive. For instance, any company that is crazy enough to spend millions on a Super Bowl ad is actually sending a message by that fact alone—because everybody knows how expensive those ads are.

If you've watched the Super Bowl, an NBA playoff game, the Olympics, or some other expensive advertising event, you may have occasionally noticed a commercial for Boeing. You may think, "Why are they trying to sell me an airplane? I can barely afford the payments on my pickup truck!" The answer is, that's not what they're selling—at least directly. And they're not talking to you, so get off the couch and get your buddies another beer. No, they're selling confidence in Boeing to the tiny handful of customers and investors who are also watching the Super Bowl (that is, if not from their own private box). The practical side of you may ask, "Well why don't they just take these people to lunch directly since there are so few of them?" They probably do that, too. But running an ad during the Super Bowl makes a supremely confident impression. Besides whatever advertising message is scripted into the ad about Boeing's products and commitment to human values, etc., is the not-so-subtle subtext, "Look how well we're doing! We can afford a Super Bowl commercial!"

CEOs of airlines, members of select Congressional committees, investment analysts, and fund managers all have a pretty good idea of how much a Super Bowl ad costs. That fact alone makes as much an impression on them as the Alexander Amosu suit the CEO of Boeing may wear to lunch with them. Of course, the CEO of Boeing could wear a tan J. C. Penney sports coat to that lunch, but he's not going to project the same level of confidence and success as the Amosu. (In truth, since we're making this up, the CEO of Boeing probably wears something in between a Penney and an Amosu. Maybe a nice Armani?)

But getting back to the seeming uselessness of a Boeing commercial during the Super Bowl, it's not that the commercial is particularly creative or that its message is memorable, it's that being a sponsor of the Super Bowl projects an image of success. And that underscores the emotional confidence that a prospective buyer or investor has in going with Boeing over Airbus. The sheer price of the medium, in this case, is the message. Or it might also say "We're nuts."

On a less lofty scale, these days, a company that is on Facebook or Twitter is saying that it's hip and relevant. It's totally with it, dude. But if the messages it tweets aren't strong and provocative, even Twitter won't help it. A boring story is a boring story, no matter what the medium. And media-over-message marketing decisions are, like the term "hip," so transitory that their impact fades as quickly as the "hipness" of the medium. Remember the term, "As seen on TV"? Tomorrow's will be "Follow us on Facebook."

Likewise, on a personal marketing level, someone who is unsure of themselves can conceal his shyness by the clothes he wears, the car he drives, or some other shallow signal of self-worth. These personal accoutrements act like a medium. Someone driving a Maserati, wearing an Armani suit, or signing his restaurant bill with a Montblanc pen, is going to convey a certain aura of success and power, even though he may be an idiot. Of course, the idiocy won't be able to hide itself behind the medium of the suit for long. But the medium may give him some time to fake it.

So breaking Rule #4, letting the medium trump the message, may be allowed in certain, limited circumstances. Of course, if you can do both, make a big impression with both the medium and the message, and do it creatively, you've become a black belt marketer.

WHEN TO BREAK RULE #5, "WORK HARD TO KEEP IT SIMPLE"

This rule, like the Creativity Rule #3, would, on the surface, seem to offer no opportunities to ignore. "Keeping it simple" is such an inherently obvious virtue that it is hard to think of anytime it wouldn't apply. Of course, as we pointed out, the act of keeping a brand simple often involves complex details. It's like getting a spacecraft to Saturn. Going to Saturn is the simple idea; how you do it is a little more complicated.

But are there any instances where a brand itself should be complicated? Well, suppose you want to hide the brand? A holding company of a group of popular consumer brands would not necessarily want to make that fact obvious. For instance it wouldn't do its packaged goods brands any good for food giant ConAgra to simplify all of its brands like Hunts, Swiss Miss, Chef Boyardee, and dozens of others into one, overwhelming ConAgra brand. In fact, in order to keep any possible political or social controversy separate from its corporate governance, it serves ConAgra well to keep the totality of its owned brands separate and complicated. It can then use its corporate brand, ConAgra, to speak only to the investment and governmental community.

In the 1980s, out of either corporate egotism or a bad drug experience, holding company Beatrice ran an expensive ad campaign to try to explain to everybody that all of those hundred or so brands they loved were really Beatrice. Established brands like Avis, Arrowhead Water, Altoids, Butterball Turkeys, Dannon Yogurt, Orville Redenbacher's Popcorn, Playtex, Peter Pan Peanut Butter, Samsonite—all Beatrice. Not only did no one give a damn, but the campaign backfired by highlighting the impersonal, corporate nature of brands that had, up until then, become more personal. Large chunks of Beatrice ended up in the hands of ConAgra, who wasn't particularly so eager to simplify its brand.

Another example of purposefully complicating a brand is in the financial services industry. In an era of deregulation and more and more complicated financial products and instruments, it actually serves the purposes of investment banks to complicate their product brands to hide the thread of ownership. Collateralized debt obligations (CDOs) are bundled into branded tranches, sold, chopped up, retranched, and resold, each time rebranded again to hide the trail. It's like a shell game. The purpose, in this case, is not to build customer loyalty to a particular branded fund, but to avoid customer (and regulatory) scrutiny. It's marketing turned on its head.

We're not saying that any of this is right. We're just saying that, for the purposes of hiding, shall we say, certain controversial business activities, it might be useful to complicate your brand. But that's between you and your lawyers, and maybe the SEC.

But are there any above-board reasons you'd want to complicate your brand? Yes, as a matter of fact. It is well known that packaged goods companies like Procter & Gamble, Kellogg's, Unilever, and Frito Lay often put out products that would, on the surface, compete with each other. Procter and Gamble, for instance, packages five brands of laundry soap; Tide, Cheer, Bold, Gain, and Dreft. It may be argued by chemists that these are all the same; basically detergent with some perfume. But for marketing purposes, it is important to have a detergent that serves the different emotional needs of various types of customers. In fact, each product brand has spent years and millions in crafting its image and chemistry to match the emotional chemistry of its loyal customer base. Rather than competing with each other, the P&G detergents all offer a choice to a wide variety of customers; some friendly to colors, some made for stains, some safe for infants. It beats pounding your clothes on a rock by the stream.

It is the same reason that a car manufacturer like Toyota would make both Toyota and Lexus. Aren't they all just Toyotas? Not to a Lexus driver. It has been argued, for instance, that a fully loaded Toyota Camry at $36,000 MSRP is essentially the same car as a $42,000 Lexus ES; same drive train, same chassis, same body, same dashboard. But there is a difference, and it's the logo on the front of the hood. That logo says so much more about the success, and therefore personal branding, of the driver. So in this case, creating two brands for Toyota actually serves both it and its two customer groups well.

But within the boundary of a single brand, it can be generally said that integrity and simplicity should reign. Once you get to managing the individual brand's emotional relationship with a customer, keep that part simple.

WHEN TO IGNORE RULE #6, "GIVE LOVE TO GET LOVE"

Would there ever be an instance when you wouldn't want to show that you love your customers, or your employees, or you own product? Again, this seems like one of those unbreakable Unbreakable Rules like the Brand Simplicity Rule #5. Of course you would always want to love the people that make your very existence on the planet possible.

But Rule #6 is really about recognizing the general principle that giving love gets love back. (Some people, sadly, are just incapable of giving love back. But forget them.) Much as Rule #2 is about recognizing that for your customers, their perceptions are reality, there can be circumstances where a better opportunity would arise from not showing love for your customer…at least universal love.

Take the brand of the United States Marines. Their message used to be, "We're looking for a few good men." That's evolved to the current, "The Few. The Proud. The Marines." Now it is generally recognized that the one thing a Marine loves most is a fellow Marine. The bond of loyalty and affection among the employees of the USMC is perhaps unequaled by any other organization on earth. So the employees really love each other. And they love their company, the USMC. And their company demonstrably loves them right back. It's one big love fest—if you're a Marine.

But outsiders? The potential recruits of the Marines? The ones their advertising campaigns speak to? Not so much. In fact, there is almost an air of contempt, a challenge to these not-yet Marines that they probably aren't good enough to be one of The Few. This contempt is consciously designed to provoke an emotional response: "Oh yeah? I am, too, good enough!" The brand promise of the Marines is that if you can take what they dish out in hardship, insult, and pain, you may be allowed into one of the most elite clubs in the world. And then you earn your love. In this case, it pays to break the universal love rule, in favor of the Love-Only-Marines Rule.

Of course, the ultimate "customer" of the Marine Corps is the American taxpayer, on whose behalf this band of elite warriors storms beaches and plants flags on volcanoes. The marketing message of the Marines to the rest of America isn't exactly love—at least not love like they show each other—but it is love of the same thing that the taxpayer loves, the United States. And the desired effect on that taxpaying customer, while not necessarily feeling the love of the Marine Corps, is at least the relief that they are on "our side."

Other organizations may find it useful to use this "Are you good enough?" message, in order to recruit employees or customers. In these cases, whether it's for a gym, a country club, or an expensive brand of clothing, it is important to show conditional love; love that you earn. Even some expensive restaurants, whose business you would think depends on fawning service, choose to behave snooty to customers they don't recognize as making the cut, so that the patrons that do make the cut feel even more special to have even gotten onto the reservation book. But as with the Marines, the elect who are seated feel an earned love, even though their "earning" it may merely come from being rich or famous.

On a personal marketing level, many relationships are formed between people who make it difficult to love them. They develop a personal brand of being taciturn, or cranky, or just hard to please. The sometimes perverse result is that the person who earns the love of another "impossible" person really values it more than if it is easily given. Again we're not saying this is right. But we have to recognize that it's a branding technique that is built on breaking the Give Love to Get Love Rule.

But ultimately, love is in there at the end. You may have to make them earn it. You may make them crawl through cold mud under live ammo and barbed wired. You may make them put up with a lot of insult and abuse. But in the end, love better be the reward. So you can't ignore it completely.

WHEN TO BREAK RULE #7, "EMOTIONS RULE THE WORLD"

This may seem like an easy rule to break. Companies marketing to scientists, engineers, or cold-hearted business people, believe that emotions play no part in their calculations.

Of course, as we've seen, this is a myth. Everyone is emotional, even scientists. If someone says he's not emotional, bring up a topic you know will make his face red. Even the most critical of engineers will be moved by an emotional approach, though it is decorated with data. Different stimuli evoke different emotions in different types of people. The trick is to find the right emotion for the audience and poke that.

But there may be instances where, even for otherwise emotionally volatile people, a non-emotional tactic, one that goes directly for the left brain, would be better.

Advertising for scientific instruments seems to do this. Users of these instruments claim that they are only influenced by cold, hard specs. So once you have their attention, it's time to drop the emotional manipulation and just get to the facts. Make them laugh, but then respect their time and need for data by serving up the info pronto.

Even the marketing of consumer products has a place where you drop the emotional appeal and go directly to information. The place to do this is usually when the emotional appeal has worked and the customer has arrived at your website looking for information. At that stage what they need is not more feeling but some clear, measurable facts to reinforce the emotional decision that got them to your site to begin with. They're in information-seeking mode. So give it to them. Make it easy to find. Give them as much data as they need to confirm their decision to like you. This is the time when you let up on Rule #7.

Ever look down the cereal aisle of a supermarket and see people trying to read the ingredients on the side of a box of

Cheerios? Ever watch people who've decided to buy a car pore over the technical specs at the back of a brochure? Or have you ever gone to a brand's website for more information? That's when you move from emotional to rational with your marketing.

Some companies don't know when to stop marketing and just shut up. You go to their websites, intrigued by an ad, perhaps, or already sold on the brand, just to look for information. Only it's impossible to find. Instead, on every page you wade through more and more "sales talk" until you're ready to give up and walk out...or log off.

Year ago, long before the age of Wikipedia, Jeff wanted to buy an *Encyclopedia Britannica* for his kids. Back during the Late Pleistocene Jeff had grown up and gone to school with the *Britannica*, the twenty-three volumes groaning on his own dad's bookcase, and he wanted his kids to have the same resource. He was already sold on the brand. Emotionally he was right where the *Britannica* brand would want him.

So he went to a local chain bookstore in a mall where he had seen a *Britannica* booth and announced to the salesman he wanted to buy one. But in those days you just couldn't "buy" an *Encyclopedia Britannica*, you had to go through the "sales process." Apparently some marketing VP at EB had determined that there would always be resistance to buying an encyclopedia (they weren't cheap, costing and weighing about as much, at the time, as a small car), so the publisher set up this long, complicated, marketing process of overcoming that anticipated resistance.

Yet here was a guy who was already sold. He was

resistance-free. He was ready to pay cash for the whole thing; even had his checkbook out. But *Encyclopedia Britannica's* marketing machine wouldn't let him just buy one to save his life. All the sales representative in the store could do was make a spiel (that didn't need to be made) and set him up with an appointment for a *Britannica* salesman to come to his home. Jeff thought, okay, fine; he really wanted to get an encyclopedia—you know, for the kids. So he set up the appointment.

When the home salesman came he insisted on taking Jeff through a lavish, expensively produced brochure extolling the glorious virtues of the *Encyclopedia Britannica* and what it could do for his children's opportunities. Jeff cut him off and said he was already sold, ready to order right now, write the check, everything. But the home sales associate was not allowed to go there. He was there to overcome resistance to the sale but not authorized to close the sale himself. That needed a more senior sales person, apparently. He left the glossy brochure with Jeff but with no mechanism to buy it. Nowhere in the brochure was there an order form or even a phone number to call to get one. The associate was, however, empowered to make an appointment for another, authorized salesman come by at a later date to set up the actual contract, once Jeff had a chance to talk it over with his family around the kitchen table.

Frustrated, Jeff finally gave up on his dream of owning a *Britannica*. He wrote a letter to the president of EB in Chicago advising her to go down the hall to her VP of Marketing and fire him. He told her she had lost a sure sale by over-selling. Fortunately for the Berry family, the Internet came along by the time Jeff's offspring were old enough to use an encyclopedia, so he not only saved $3,800, he also saved himself about quarter of a ton and six bookcase-feet of useless paper.

In the end of this tale of counter-productive marketing, emotions actually did rule after all; the wrong ones. The lesson is not to ignore the "Emotions Rule" rule, but to know at what point to drop appealing to the emotions and be ready with information. And with an order form.

Break Rule#7 when the sale is primed and ready. Once you get people's attention, be ready with information. Or get ready for the wrong kind of emotion.

WHEN TO BREAK RULE #8, "GO BIG OR GO HOME"

This is a tricky one. Of course, on the surface, you'd expect to need to go all out in everything you do. Either play 100% (or 110% as high school coaches like to say) or don't play at all. In actual life, though, if you played at 100% nonstop throughout every game, much less 110%, you'd fall down exhausted before the half. You train yourself to sprint when you have to and rest when you don't. The 100% really applies to attention, not to physical effort. Go big with brains, not brawn.

It would be reasonable, for instance, to hold off with an ad campaign until your manufacturing, distribution, sales, and customer service operations are ready to handle the extra load. Effective ad campaigns have actually killed companies that couldn't handle the sudden demand. So make sure your whole organization is ready to support your marketing promise. Go big in a balanced, coordinated way, or go home in pieces.

Going big means that the goal is constantly in sight, even when the means are lagging. You may have to start small because of funds or resources, but don't forget to ramp up when the momentum builds and those resources finally come in. While it's important not to flood the engine by mashing down the accelerator, it's equally important, when gathering speed, to keep applying the pressure.

We said this was tricky. Maybe the best way to address breaking this rule is to think of your marketing as a football team. A successful team reads the field, reads the opponent, reads the conditions and adjusts its tactics accordingly. If every play ran straight up through the middle, it would be the easiest team to beat. Obeying Rule #8 means going all out with your thinking and skill, but with your eye constantly on the ultimate goal. It doesn't mean pounding your head against an immovable object until it moves.

WHEN TO BREAK RULE #9, "EVERYTHING IS MARKETING"

This one is easy: Never.

Of all of the rules, this one is the most unbreakable. Every little thing you do, with your company or yourself, sends a marketing message. In life and in business there is no off-season. Everything counts. Every little thing makes an impression.

If someone is not your customer, you are still marketing to

them even if you don't think they're likely to be a customer. They are either a potential customer or they will know someone who is. So, for instance, if you develop a reputation for quality or good service or integrity, that reputation will influence people who eventually are in a position to be your customer. You never know. On the other hand, if you let your inattention to little things create an impression of sloppiness, rudeness, greediness, or contempt, you are also influencing potential customers. Think of marketing as existing in a kind of universal force field of everyone's opinions. How you behave, even on the smallest level, resonates against that field and affects opinions. Nothing you do exists in a vacuum.

Remember, you're on stage all the time. People are watching you and forming silent judgments. It's not fair, but there it is. So give them reasons to admire you and your company, even when you're having a bad day.

In short, Rule# 9 is the one rule that is truly never, ever, ever, ever, ever, ever breakable.

CAN'T GET AROUND THEM

Everything has a breaking point, even supposedly unbreakable rules. But we all know that the real world isn't so black and white. The Ten Commandments, for instance, are supposedly unbreakable rules—that's why they're called "commandments." But if you were hiding Anne Frank's family in your attic and the Gestapo came around, of course you would break the commandment against lying (unless you were a sanctimonious monster). But you would do so to avoid committing a more serious sin, namely causing the death of innocent people. Likewise, if aliens were to demand that you commit adultery with Scarlett Johansson (or Ryan Reynolds if you're of that persuasion) or they'd destroy the planet, of course you'd make the sacrifice and break that commandment…for the greater good. Everything depends on context.

But context or not, the Commandments are there. And so are the Unbreakable Rules of Marketing. You can choose to ignore them. You can rationalize breaking them. You can even flip them off. But you can't get around them.

Think first.

>DO THIS

Know when to break the rules and why.

LET'S REVIEW, SHALL WE?

THE SHORT COURSE

For those of you who are too impatient to read the entire book and need the Short Attention Span version (something you could easily read on a plane ride between Portland and Seattle), we are offering you the convenience of turning back to the end here and ticking off The 9½ Unbreakable Rules. Of course, you run the risk of missing some of the important nuances, not to mention the juicy case studies, guru-like observations about life, and knee-slapping humor. But, as we ourselves want to obey Rule #6 and love our readers, here is a short summary of all 9½ Unbreakable Rules of Marketing.

RULE #1: CONSISTENCY BEATS ABILITY

Here's a sad truth: over the long term, a company that is consistent with its marketing message is going to whip a competitor who changes its message constantly, even though some of those messages may occasionally be compelling, creative, and clever.

Of course, if you can also manage to be compelling, creative, and clever, and do it consistently, that's the best of all worlds. But if you can only manage to be good all the time, let your competitor be occasionally excellent. You'll still beat him.

RULE #2: PERCEPTION IS REALITY

People rarely let the facts get in the way of their beliefs. In fact, people are quite skilled at cherry-picking facts to support what they already believe to be true.

If you can get in at the head of that cherry-picking and influence your customers' beliefs about you, leave all the rationalization work to them. You should, of course, be ready with just enough facts to support their perception, but once they see you a certain way, it will take a major force of nature to pry them away from that perception. And facts have nothing to do with it.

Perception is what motivates behavior, not reality. Reality is just a perception that a group of people agree on.

RULE #3: BE CREATIVE OR DIE

Nobody ever bored their customers into buying their products. You absolutely have to be creative to get through and to make your message sink in. This is the soul of effective marketing.

Creativity often means entertainment. Remember that all marketing messages are interruptions. So if you interrupt someone, you'd better make it worth their while, if nothing else but to keep them from fast-forwarding right through your commercial. So entertain. Use humor. Use pathos. Use intrigue. But don't bore.

Boredom is death, at least for you.

RULE #4: THE MEDIUM IS NOT THE MESSAGE

If your message is strong, memorable, and entertaining, it doesn't matter what medium you use to send it. It will find its own way. Of course, it helps to actually post it, broadcast it, or print it, but there is no single, magical medium that will make it go viral. The magic that does that is the message itself.

Revolutions have been and are still being started by a powerful message: freedom and equality. Great brands have been launched and grown the same way, by a single resonant message. And it hasn't mattered if the message was announced by a multi-million dollar TV campaign, by Twitter, by Facebook, or by word of mouth; the strong message always gets through. It finds a way.

RULE #5: WORK HARD TO KEEP IT SIMPLE

Your marketing should be simple. It should be something that could be described in a Tweet. It should be instantly understood and recognizable at high speed on a freeway, and summed up by every employee without hesitation. Complicated is forgettable; simple is memorable.

But keeping your marketing simple is hard. It requires endless editing, obsessive paring down, and never-ending diligence. It also requires self-discipline to keep it simple and to keep from junking it up with clauses, after-thoughts, and add-ons.

Just stick to the point.

RULE #6: GIVE LOVE TO GET LOVE

Success in business is ultimately reciprocal. It boils down to the simple maxim: If you love your customers, they're more likely to love you back. And it goes without saying, of course, that they're more likely to want to buy from you.

But you can't give lip service to this idea. You have to really love your customers. Love isn't a feeling: it's action. You do it in every detail of the way you run your business. It shows in everything from your advertising to the way you craft your products on the factory floor. And you do it from the way you treat your employees to the way they, in turn, want to pass that love on to your customers.

It's as simple as that.

RULE #7: EMOTIONS RULE THE WORLD

Facts and figures will never motivate people like emotions. An emotional reaction to a stimulus takes milliseconds, while conscious processing of the same stimulus can take several minutes. The emotional reaction wins by a mile. By the time a person is thinking about their options, they're already looking for reasons to back up what their heart has decided.

Win people over emotionally and they'll take care of the reasons. Make them laugh. Scare them. Make them cry. Make them hungry. Make them envious. In fact, do anything besides putting them to sleep and they'll be in your complete control.

RULE #8: GO BIG OR GO HOME

Great marketing messages aren't magic spells. You can't come up with the perfect, creative message, whisper it in secret ceremony at midnight, and expect the customers to start flocking to your website. You have to shout it from the rooftops—or at least on YouTube.

Marketing requires that you go all out. Don't just talk to your existing customers, talk to all of those customers you don't have yet. Talk to everybody. Your employees, your channel, your shareholders, your suppliers, the press, even your mom all have to be able to repeat your message in their sleep. They should not be able to get it out of their heads.

Weak marketing gets you nothing. Strong marketing, using every ounce of effort, is unstoppable.

RULE #9: EVERYTHING IS MARKETING

Marketing isn't something that's done separately by your marketing department. Everything you do is marketing. It includes how you design and make your products. It includes the manner in which you sell them. It includes how you run your company, how you treat your employees, how you treat your customers, how the public sees you. It even comes down to how your receptionist answers the phone or how you sign your e-mails.

Everything you do makes an impression. And every impression you make is marketing.

THE ½ RULE: KNOW THE RULES AND KNOW WHEN TO BREAK THEM

It's sometimes right to break one of the Unbreakable Rules. But know what rule you are breaking and why. Whether it's a tactical or strategic reason, or you are just willfully ignoring it, make sure that the downside to breaking one of the Unbreakable 9 is outweighed by the net upside to your overall marketing. And the upside is never because it's just convenient. Or that it's too hard.

Come to think of it, you should probably ask our permission first.

And you'd better have a good reason.

ANY QUESTIONS?

SUGGESTED READING AND VIEWING

AUTHOR/DIRECTOR	TITLE	DATE
Conway, Jack (Dir)	*The Hucksters* (a timeless film about marketing)	1947
Ellis, David (Dir)	*Snakes on a Plane* (film)	2006
Gladwell, Malcolm	*The Tipping Point:* *How Little Things Can* *Make a Big Difference*	2000
Gladwell, Malcolm	*Blink: The Power of Thinking* *Without Thinking*	2005
Heath, Dan & Chip	*Made to Stick:* *Why Some Ideas* *Survive and Others Die*	2007
Lehrer, Jonah	*How We Decide*	2009
McLuhan, Marshall	*Understanding Media;* *the Extensions of Man*	1964
Ogilvy, David	*Confessions of an* *Advertising Man*	1963
Pinker, Steven	*How the Mind Works*	1997
Pinker, Steven	*Blank Slate:* *The Modern Denial* *of Human Nature*	2002
Plassman, Doherty, Shiv, Rangel	**"Marketing actions can** **modulate neural representations** **of experienced pleasantness"** *Proceedings of the* *National Academy of Sciences*	Dec 2007
Pray, Douglas (Dir)	*Art & Copy* (documentary film)	2009
Schwartz, Barry	*"The Tyranny of Choice"* Scientific American	Apr 2004
Zameckis, Robert (Dir)	*Cast Away* (film as a marketing message)	2000

INDEX

CPSIA information can be obtained
at www.ICGtesting.com
Printed in the USA
FSHW011611011119
63621FS